Against the Odds

An evaluation of chi
family support servic

Ger information ☏ 016... ...Williamson

JR
JOSEPH
ROWNTREE
FOUNDATION

NATIONAL
CHILDREN'S
BUREAU
making a difference

The National Children's Bureau promotes the interests and well-being of all children and young people across every aspect of their lives. NCB advocates the participation of children and young people in all matters affecting them. NCB challenges disadvantage in childhood.

NCB achieves its mission by
- ensuring the views of children and young people are listened to and taken into account at all times
- playing an active role in policy development and advocacy
- undertaking high quality research and work from an evidence based perspective
- promoting multidisciplinary, cross-agency partnerships
- identifying, developing and promoting good practice
- disseminating information to professionals, policy makers, parents and children and young people

NCB has adopted and works within the UN Convention on the Rights of the Child.

Several Councils and Fora are based at NCB and contribute significantly to the breadth of its influence. It also works in partnership with Children in Scotland and Children in Wales and other voluntary organisations concerned for children and their families.

The Joseph Rowntree Foundation has supported this project as part of its programme of research and innovative development projects, which it hopes will be of value to policy makers and practitioners.

The views expressed in this book are those of the authors and not necessarily those of the National Children's Bureau or the Joseph Rowntree Foundation.

Published by National Children's Bureau Enterprises Ltd, the trading company for the National Children's Bureau, Registered Charity number 258825. 8 Wakley Street, London EC1V 7QE. Tel: 020 7843 6000

© National Children's Bureau and Joseph Rowntree Foundation, 2002
Published 2002

ISBN 1 900990 14 8

British Library Cataloguing in Publication Data
A catalogue record for this book is available from the British Library

Typeset by LaserScript, Surrey
Printed and bound by Page Bros, Norwich

Contents

List of tables and figures

Acknowledgements

The impetus for this research came from the social services department in which the study took place, mindful of the fact that it was often having to make decisions about its service profile in the absence of information on the effectiveness of its services. Staff and managers alike shared this concern, albeit to some extent with different stakeholder interests, and we are deeply grateful to staff, as well as to service users, for their participation in this study. Like service users, staff were open, frank and gave unstintingly of their time over a two-year period. They were, from the outset, concerned to improve their practice, and keen to develop routine ways of more rigorously evaluating their own work. We hope that this study will contribute to both developments.

Thanks are also due to members of the study's steering committee, Martin Knapp, Nina Biehal, Owen Gill and Collette McAuley. Richard Dixon also made his contribution to the project. Susan Taylor of the Joseph Rowntree Foundation provided constant support and encouragement and, with Jane Brotchie (Editorial Consultant) was instrumental in helping us to bring this project to its conclusion and in preparing what we hope will be a readable account. If it is not, the fault lies only with ourselves.

1. Introduction

The importance of developing an evidence-based approach to decision-making and service provision in the public sector is a major concern of Government and of local authority social services departments (see Davies and others, 1994; Smith, 1996; NHS Centre for Reviews and Dissemination, 2000). The study described in this volume was one of a number of projects funded by the Joseph Rowntree Foundation in an effort to address a gap in our knowledge relating to child and family support (see, for example, Biehal and others, 2000).

The scope of the research study

This study points to some of the challenges facing those who seek to make evidence-based social services a reality. It will interest anyone concerned with the future of child and family support services, particularly practitioners and middle and senior managers who are developing policy and practice in this field.

The report offers a detailed look at how child and family support services are working in one local authority, giving a valuable insight into what workers are doing on a day-to-day basis and some of the tensions inherent in the work. It explores the success of the service in preventing the removal of children from their families, and in resolving the problems experienced by children and families, including problems relating to school exclusion. The study also looks at whether or not families referred to this child and family support service were being offered the right kind of help at the right time, and whether or not there were missed opportunities to help at an early stage in the development of problems.

Children and families talk about what they value about the service and the report draws some conclusions about how services can be developed so as to make the most of the best practice that was identified in the study. Key practice issues are identified. Although some of these issues are complex, the report focuses on a number of clear suggestions for improvements, based on the findings, that can be applied to practice. These suggestions are likely to be relevant to child and family support services around the country as well as to the one that was the focus of this study.

The use and abuse of research

The study does not provide unequivocal evidence of the effectiveness or ineffective-ness of child and family support services. Methodologically (given the eventual shape of the project) it can do neither. What this research *does* do is to point to a number of key issues that social services (together with health and education) should consider if they are to take a responsible and accountable approach to service delivery.

Research of this kind places social workers and their departments under detailed scrutiny and it requires considerable courage to expose one's policies and practices in this way. It is anxiety provoking, intrusive and entails additional work for staff. It also carries risks. For example, you will find the data reveal that some workers were not operating in a way that could be described as 'evidence-based'. It would be rather surprising if they all were, since we are still finding out what is needed to support such a working culture. Rather than blaming staff for not getting it right, this suggests a need for a more considered and informed approach to service devel-opment. It points also to the need for a better social services department infrastructure that can actively promote an evidence-based approach to policy and practice.

Charged with the goals of preventing out-of-home care for those children already at serious risk of such a move, along with other, equally onerous responsibilities, it appears that child and family support services are working with the odds stacked against them. This study found that the service was highly valued by the families, even though their problems were not always resolved. The question is not whether the services are needed – they clearly are – but what we can legitimately expect from these services in terms of substantial change when they are working with limited resources and time constraints. This is particularly true given the long-stand-ing and complex problems that typify most families referred to the child and family support service.

It was clear from the outset of this research that the local authority in question was looking to make serious cuts in its child care budget, together with many departments throughout the UK. At the same time it was trying to comply with government initiatives such as *Quality Protects* (Department of Health, 1998). This is the very context that those concerned with the potentially negative impact of an 'evidence-based culture' are so worried about. It is the fear that lack of evidence of effectiveness will be re-interpreted (or interpreted) as evidence of ineffectiveness. Indeed, the way in which such research is used is a test of the 'evidence-based maturity' of the social services department and of its political leadership.

However carefully or cautiously research findings are presented one can never be certain how they will be perceived and used by others. It is a disheartening fact that the social services department that initiated this research has subsequently used parts of the study as a justification for cutting back a service that was already under-resourced. Such actions can only fuel people's suspicions that evaluative evidence will be used to undermine staff efforts rather than, as staff hoped, be used as a means to improve practice and to develop ways of rigorously evaluating their work.

Although it cannot help individuals whose posts have already been cut, and families who will miss the help they provided, we hope that this volume will go some way to counterbalance such unfortunate outcomes and contribute to more positive developments in the future of preventive services for children and families in other parts of the UK.

2. Evaluating child and family support services

This chapter introduces the work of child and family support services (CFSS) and their contribution to preventive social services. It discusses some of the challenges inherent in evaluating the services and how the researchers addressed these in this project. More detail about the research methodology is supplied in the appendices.

Preventive services

A key principle of the Children Act 1989 is that families in need should have access to services which enable them adequately to care for their children, and that local authority social services should work to prevent the need for children to be accommodated in public care whenever possible. One of the service options available to pursue these aims is the provision of family centres. Family centres provide a range of services to families, the detail of which varies, depending on how they relate to other services available within a department. They are broadly preventive, encompassing work with individuals, couples and families, crisis intervention and groupwork.

Preventive services potentially operate at two levels:

- To prevent the development of problems that might give rise to children becoming the subject of child protection or educational concerns.
- To address problems that have already arisen and which place children at risk of out-of-home placement or school exclusion, both of which can have serious consequences for a young person's future well-being. Examples of problems which may place children at risk of out-of-home placement include family breakdown, parental abuse or neglect, parent–adolescent conflict, substance misuse, mental health, domestic violence or juvenile delinquency. In the latter context, child and family support services are often referred to as 'family preservation services'. There is a substantial North American literature on the effectiveness

of family preservation services, but relatively little evaluative work has been undertaken within the UK (see Macdonald and Williamson, 2001).

Measures of effectiveness

The effectiveness of child and family support services (CFSS) is often measured solely in terms of their success in avoiding the out-of-home placement of those children thought to be at risk of entering them. Studies conducted primarily in North America have cumulatively drawn attention to a number of problems associated with such an approach to service evaluation. Two issues are particularly significant:

- **Factors associated with out-of-home placement are complex.** Where controlled studies have been conducted the results are at best ambiguous. Children in control groups rarely have higher rates of placement than those in receipt of family preservation services, suggesting either that family preservation services are no more effective than the routine services against which they are usually compared, or that social workers and others are unable to identify those families at serious risk of breakdown.
- **Placement prevention is a dubious good if children are left in risky situations or in situations where their welfare is inadequately ensured.** In other words, workers and evaluators should pay more attention to changes in the family environment. This encompasses adequate housing and resources, parenting adequacy, family functioning and the amelioration of problems within the family such as maternal depression, substance misuse and child behaviour problems.

Even when we have data on the outcomes for children and families to whom support services have been provided, these need careful interpretation because:

- **We know little about which service 'ingredients' are particularly effective with which families in which circumstances, or what kinds of families, problems or circumstances are more likely to result in poor outcomes.** Indeed, we know relatively little about precisely what is provided to troubled children and families (Fraser and others, 1991; Wells and Biegal, 1991). Although some preliminary work has been done in North America and in the UK (see Gibbons and others, 1990) we need to know more about the scope, quality and provision of services which fall under the heading 'Child and Family Support'. Such information is necessary if we are to find out which strands of service provision are most effective with which service users, and what factors conspire to undermine or enhance effectiveness. This was a major focus of this study.

■ **Some difficulties may be so entrenched that a short-term intervention, however intense and however appropriate, may be insufficient to effect substantial change.** This study explored the potential impact of refocusing resources earlier in the development of family and child problems.

The evaluation study

Given the complex nature of evaluation in this field, and the problems identified by previous researchers, this study had three inter-related aims:

■ To provide a detailed profile of the recipients of Child and Family Support Services (CFSS) and of services provided for them.
■ To examine the relationship of the above profile and services to intended and unintended service outcomes, including out-of-home placement.
■ To explore the scope for the refocusing of services towards early prevention.

Limits of the study

The final design of this study is rather different from that originally envisaged. A planned comparison group 'disappeared' when the social services department reorganised shortly after the study commenced. We encountered further difficulties in accessing families when workers were concerned that such contact would jeopardise the work they were seeking to do, or would be too stressful for the family. Some of the complexity of the study design (see Appendices 1, 2 and 3) is a result of our endeavours to secure compensatory information when planned avenues of inquiry ran into difficulties.

The study is exploratory. It was not designed to provide a definitive answer to the question: 'Do these services work?' The absence of a control group means that we simply cannot know what the outcomes for these families would have been had they not received help from this service. Therefore, it does not provide information on which to base decisions on the continuation of the service. The final design might more accurately be described as a process evaluation, rather than an outcome study.

What the research *does* do is to present a detailed picture about who is doing what, with whom, where and in what ways, with what outcomes. It provides information about the appropriateness of the kinds of interventions provided within the service, the factors which help or hinder progress, the appropriateness of referrals and how staff and service users see its effectiveness. Such information is pertinent in deciding on the development of services, eligibility criteria for services, and so on. It is to the future development of preventive services for children and families that this project is directed.

Data collection

The study collected information from five sources. These are described in more detail in Appendix 1.

- A content analysis of the records of 152 families who had received help from the child and family support service and whose cases were closed between November 1997 and November 1998 (in relation to that service).
- A one group pre-test post-test evaluation of the child and family support services. Two sets of data contributed towards this: interviews with social workers and interviews with service users.
- Background interviews with all family centre staff, to elicit general information about factors which we thought might influence service delivery.
- An analysis of the working agreements, reviews and closing summaries of those cases referred to the service, including those where we had not been able to interview the family.
- An analysis of data available from the management information system to identify what had subsequently happened to children in relation to placements or exclusion from school, whether or not cases remained opened to social services or were closed, whether or not the child's name was placed on or removed from the child protection register.

3. Profile of the study area, staff and families

The study area

The study area is a city in the south-west of England. Child and family support services are provided by four teams, each of which is managed by a Project Officer. The teams operate across six family centres, five of which are located within the social services department, the other being a voluntary sector family centre from which the City Council contracts a certain amount of service. The centres each serve a defined geographical area. Referrals from schools and locality team social workers are screened against pre-specified criteria either by project officers (the teams managed by social services) or, in the case of the voluntary sector centre, by a panel comprising representatives from education and social services.

The following children are the main target groups.

The criteria for working with children

The teams are expected to target their resources at the following groups of children:

- those at imminent risk of family breakdown leading to a child's admission to local authority accommodation
- children admitted to local authority accommodation within the last four weeks, and there is a plan to return the child home
- a child who is excluded or at risk of exclusion or serious self exclusion from school *and* contributory family difficulties of significant and serious concern.

If resources permit:

- children in long term accommodation in public care where there is a risk of breakdown
- children in long term accommodation where there is a reunification plan with the family of origin or reconstructed family (child looked after more than four weeks).

This service represents an important contribution to the preventive work of the social services department. As with other social services departments in the UK, the Government is encouraging a refocusing of resources towards preventive and supportive services and away from heavier, investigative approaches characteristic of child care social work in the 1990s (Rose, 1994; Department of Health, 1994; Parton, 1997). It also plays an important part in facilitating the reunification of children who have been placed in out-of-home placements.

Special expertise

The child and family support teams combine the expertise of social work and teaching. The difficulties which children have in school sometimes reflect difficulties they are experiencing at home. The threat or reality of school exclusion is a frequent trigger for referral to social services, as problems at home often come to light in such circumstances. Children excluded from school are more likely to become involved in delinquent or antisocial activities, including substance and alcohol misuse, and are at risk for a range of long-term adverse outcomes (Wierson and Forehand, 1994). The involvement of teachers in the child and family support service reflects the wider commitment of the social services and education departments to work collaboratively in recognition of the inter-relatedness of problems at home and problems at school.

Reorganisation of services

Shortly after the study began, the department reorganised its services. For the child and family support service, this meant a reduction from five teams operating from five family centres, to four teams working across six centres. This rationalisation of services meant that some staff had to move to a new centre, and the reduction of Project Officer (team manager) posts meant that these staff had to apply for a smaller pool of jobs within the reorganised service.

As is often the case, staff felt bruised by the way things had been handled and concerned that their services were being evaluated during such a period of flux. Worries about the timing of the research were twofold. First, would it provide an accurate picture, given the transitional (and in the views of many, the chaotic) period in which much of it took place? Secondly, how would the results be used? Most thought that if it provided a positive message of the service's worth and value it would be ignored, and if it suggested it was not value for money or was not achieving its aims, that it would be used to close the service altogether.

These concerns must be taken seriously, and the report read in this context. Our overall view is that the reorganisation did not undermine the validity of the findings of the study as a whole. This view is based on the consistency of findings over the period of the entire study, and on data from the closed cases (cases that were dealt with prior to the reorganisation).

Impact of the changes on service delivery

Historically, the child and family support service had comprised teams which operated rather differently from one another, some working more with older children, some with younger, some providing group work, others family therapy and so on. One of the driving forces for the reorganisation of the service was the desire to harmonise service provision across the city and to extend child and family services to an area previously not receiving a service. In addition to a more consistent approach to referrals, guidelines were instigated on the length of time they should expect to work with a family (before a review) and the organisation (not the content) of this work. In the interests of ensuring that service users receive a comparable service at whatever point of contact they have with the service this is laudable. There were some less desirable consequences, however, such as some staff feeling less confident in working with unfamiliar clients and problems.

Teachers faced a similar post-reorganisation challenge. Prior to reorganisation, the child and family support teachers were linked to a small number of schools within the city. Because there are only a small number of teachers, this meant that some schools did not have a link person with the child and family support service. Rather than increase the number of child and family support service teachers across the city (not possible because of resource constraints), a decision was made to share the existing number of teachers more equitably. Teachers were therefore moved from the relatively intimate one-on-one associations with *some* schools which they had come to know well and with whom they enjoyed close working relationships, and given responsibility for liaison with a larger number of schools (often not including those they had previously worked with).

As far as the teaching staff were concerned, the new organisation meant that they could no longer establish the kinds of relationships and links with head teachers and class teachers that they regarded as being so important for securing good outcomes for children in difficulty. It also meant that those relationships that had been established were rather inefficiently 'discarded'. That said, one of the project officers observed that one of the more positive consequences was that teachers' work appeared to be more child-focused and that individual work with children was enhanced. Both positions reflected personal or professional opinion, rather than anything more evidence-based.

Profile of the teams

Teams varied in size, from a team with a total staff complement of nine, to one with a staff complement of just three. Most of the workers were white and the majority were women.

The number and profile of staff varied during the course of the study as people left and joined the teams, including student social workers on placement. Overall the data testify to an experienced workforce.

Qualifications

When the background interviews were conducted, teams comprised 23 professionally qualified social workers and one unqualified social worker. Due to subsequent illness, the unqualified social worker did not participate in the study. Qualified staff typically held either the Diploma in Social Work or its predecessor, the Certificate of Qualification in Social Work. Some staff also held a Masters' qualification in Social Work or Applied Social Studies. There were six teachers seconded to the service by the education department. Five members of staff had undertaken courses leading to a further professional award, of whom two social workers and a project officer held Diplomas in Family Therapy. Two of the teachers were pursuing a Masters' degree.

Experience

Over half of the staff had been qualified for up to nine years (n=12) and just under half (n=11) had been qualified for more than nine years (range 1–30 years). Only one worker had been qualified for less than five years. Further, three quarters of all staff had worked in child and family support teams for more than one year, and almost half for more than four years.

The children and their families

Three samples have been used in this research:

- the families referred to the service during the study period (249 families);
- a smaller sample of the same families (72) who were interviewed (30 families were interviewed twice); and
- 152 families that had received the service in the past and were now on file as 'closed cases'.

During the study period 249 families were referred to the child and family support service, the majority of whom had already had three or more previous contacts with social services. Children referred to the service were predominantly male (64%). Of the girls referred to the service during the study period, 58% were white, the remainder being from minority ethnic groups, predominantly African Caribbean or Black British. However, data were missing in a significant number of cases. Even allowing for the numbers of children whose ethnic identities were not recorded, the numbers of girls from minority ethnic groups exceeded that of boys, where 85% were White British or White European.

The names of 29 children were on the child protection register at the time of referral, and a further 32 families had had children registered in the past, some on two occasions (10), and in three instances three times. However, when the scope of the child protection concerns is widened to include child protection investigations and case conferences, we find that 117 of these families had presented concerns in the past. Almost half the families had been the subject of a child protection case conference and only eight of these families had only been involved in one conference.

Profile of interviewed families

The profile of the families who were interviewed is given separately in Appendix 2. When we refer to 'views of families', these data are drawn from interviews with the 72 families referred to the service during the study period. Of these 72 families, 30 were interviewed at two points in time: shortly after referral and then after the case was closed to the child and family support service. The families interviewed were in no ways significantly different from the overall sample in relation to information provided by workers or in relation to their status in relation to child protection, placement history, and so on.

Profile of closed cases

Of the 152 families studied as 'closed cases', just over half of the children were boys, the majority of children being white (66%) and the rest being from minority ethnic groups, predominantly African Caribbean or Black British.

It is difficult to present a picture of the family composition of these families, but the evidence suggests that many of the children were living in very volatile family units. Information was not always available in the files, but where it was available the picture that emerged was one of considerable change. Thus, at first referral (to social services), 37 per cent of children were living with families where there was a step-parent present (predominantly stepfathers) and 40 per cent were living with a single parent (predominantly mothers). Just over half (52 per cent) of the total sample had at least one change of family composition and, for children whose families were referred to social services on more than one occasion, this figure rises to 76 per cent. No wonder, then, that workers identified this as an issue which made demands on their knowledge and skills.

4. Reasons for referral to child and family support services

Here we look at the problems that children and families presented to the child and family support services at the point of referral. We examine this from both the workers' and the families' perspectives. How problems are conceptualised at referral can crucially influence the kinds of intervention or service that are subsequently offered. As well as giving a flavour of the nature of the challenges presented to child and family support workers, this chapter raises important concerns about how problems are identified and how that information is recorded. This chapter needs to be read alongside the next (chapter 5) because problems are often long-standing and complex and do not fall easily into discrete categories.

As we explained earlier (chapter 2), data for this research were collected from a number of sources. This provides us with a rich resource for examining how problems are identified, described and recorded. First we consider the reasons for referral to social services and then we look at the data concerning referral to the child and family support service.

Referral to social services

Four groups played a major role as sources of referral: parents, health visitors, schools and the police. Whilst parents (predominantly mothers) were a fairly stable and major source of referrals to social services, the role of health visitors appears particularly prominent in families with very long histories of contact with the department, suggesting early concerns about adequate parenting (a concern we return to discuss in chapter 11).

What the families said

In answer to an open-ended question about problems leading to referral to social services, the families' replies were varied but specific. The majority are summarised in Table 4.1.

Families were primarily concerned about their children's behaviour, both at home and at school, and it is from this angle that most talked about problems they had in relating to young people – the relationship problems were behaviour-driven. At the same time, they were aware of the impact of other factors on their children's behaviour, such as traumas in their own lives and problems of ill health, both physical and mental. Many parents talked in particular about the impact of current and previous domestic violence on their children, the majority saying their children had witnessed domestic violence. Mental ill health and substance misuse were also concerns in about one quarter of cases. Given the numbers of children who were excluded or suspended from school (54 of the 72) and the high incidence of reported behaviour problems, this is clearly challenging work for staff to tackle.

Table 4.1 Reasons given by families for referral to social services

Reason	%	Reason	%
Housing problems	13	Physical ill health (parents)	18
Threat of eviction	6	Physical health problems (YP)	6
Financial problems/debts	14	Physical health problems (sibling)	6
Absence of utilities	6	Mental ill health (adults)	28
Conflict with neighbours	17	Mental ill health (child)	10
Racism	10	Mental ill health (sibling)	3
Social isolation	18	Substance misuse (adult)	24
School	86	Substance misuse (child)	18
Minor offences	3	Substance misuse (sibling)	3
Major offences	0	Relationship problems (adults)	18
Domestic violence	60	Relationship problems (adult/child)	79
Behaviour problems	88	Parenting	43

What the management records said (and did not say)

The social services department's records (CRISSP) give a rather more limited picture of the reasons for the referral of these same families.

The data collected in this way are neither very informative nor very accurate by comparison with the views of the families themselves. The categories used in the management information system tend to conflate reasons for referral with types of services available, with the result that the categorisation of referrals sometimes feels like constraining round pegs into square holes. At best it appears to lack a clear rationale. Such data would be more useful for the purposes of needs profiling and service planning if they were more appropriately framed and lent themselves to consistent interpretation and use.

Monitoring and evaluation is difficult without a management information system that is informative and accurate. The system in this study could be improved, for example, by clearly stating the reasons for referral, using clear categories that do not confuse 'reasons' with 'types of service'.

Figure 4.1 Reasons for most recent referral

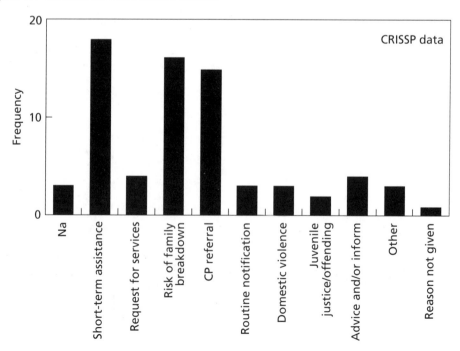

Reasons for referral to the child and family support service

One of the criteria for using the child and family support service is that the family should be at 'imminent risk of family breakdown leading to a child's admission to local authority accommodation' (see chapter 3). Our data from the working agreements, interviews with the families and with the workers help to illustrate what this might mean in practice.

What the working agreements said

The working agreement is a written record, arrived at through discussion between families and social workers. It covers what needs to change, who is seeking the changes, what the purpose of the work is, what the desired outcomes are, whether or not there is any disagreement between the parties and what the action plan is. We analysed 168 of these agreements.

'Imminent risk of family breakdown' is the single most stated reason (48 per cent) in the working agreements for referral to the child and family support service. This is followed by a combination of this *plus* school exclusion (19 per cent), with school exclusion being cited as the sole reason in some nine per cent of cases. Six children (four per cent) were in long term placements at risk of breaking down and a further 11 children (seven per cent) had recently become looked after. For these 11 children, the referral to the child and family support service was designed to facilitate their return home.

What families told us

Just under half the families thought there was a specific 'trigger' for their latest referral to social services. These might be a specific incident with the police, possible sexual abuse or parents' reactions to children such as fear of losing control and injuring children. For those who said there was 'no trigger' the problems tended to be long-standing problems with children's behaviour or school adjustment. Whilst nonetheless 'triggering' a referral at a specific point, they saw these as cumulative rather than dramatic incidents.

In just over half (55 per cent) of cases, families thought there was or had been a risk of accommodation in public care. Reasons for this are summarised in Table 4.2.

Table 4.2 Reasons given by families for perceived 'risk of accommodation'

Reason for risk of accommodation	%
Risk of physical abuse	3
Neglect / poor supervision / absent parent	8
Untenable family relationships / family breakdown	20
Risk to self	3
Unacceptable behaviour within the family	8
Unacceptable behaviour outside of the family	3
Unacceptable behaviour both inside and outside of the family	38
Mental illness	5
Other / don't know	12

Of the 11 children accommodated at the time of interview, most parents said they did not want the child returned home. Of those parents seeking accommodation, the most commonly given reasons were relationship problems between them and the child (n=6) and/or the child's behaviour (n=5). One respondent said they wanted the child punished.

> *Respondent A:* [The young person] just went berserk. [He] told them to 'f--k-off and get out of his house'. Smashed the house up and turned his music on full blast, run out in the middle of the road, giving me a load of abuse, fighting with [siblings], his sister was there as well – basically I just said to them, 'Take him away – I don't want him'.
>
> **Did they take him away?**
>
> No but we had an emergency meeting planned for the next day ... and they [field social work team] said they can't just, the boss said we can't just, we had to give it a month or something we can't just put [young person] into care regardless of what was going on so then they talked about the help.

> *Respondent B:* I asked [social services] before Christmas when he threw [his brother] off the bunk bed and done his nose. And she said 'At the moment, we'll put you through into [the child and family support service] because his father has given up on him and it'll look like you've given up on him and he'll go even more haywire'. She also said they didn't have any places, they've cut down ... I thought it would give him a break if he was with someone else on a one-to-one. The other two are so placid it's unbelievable, but lately

they're getting more anger because of what he's doing to them. So it's to give everybody a break.

Their [fieldwork team] reply was um, 'Well you can't really chuck the boy out because he's under age and basically there's nothing we can do.' They wasn't helpful at all and then my sister went up and said, 'Look she's like …' because I was in a bit of a mess and my sister said, 'Well she's just going to chuck him out so you'd best be doing something', and that was the only time they got involved. Other than that they wasn't interested. I don't find them very helpful at all.

The comments made by the last respondent show a marked lack of satisfaction with their contact with field social workers. This was in contrast to how they perceived the child and family support service workers, and is a topic that we will discuss more fully in chapter 6.

What changes did the parents hope for?

Parents were asked what would have to change in order

- for their children to be returned (if they were accommodated); or
- to make things better and to prevent the risk of out-of-home care.

Most parents cited changes in the child's behaviour (64 per cent). If school attendance, cessation of substance misuse and change of friends are included in 'behaviour change' this figure increases to 77 per cent. The remainder of changes needed were couched in terms of improvement in relationships, either parent–child (7 per cent) or adult–adult (4 per cent).

Respondent C: It wouldn't be so bad if she didn't have so much of an attitude. And a bit more consideration.

Respondent D: If I could change his dad, I'd prefer him to have him at weekends, holidays and be a normal father to him so we could calm him down, because that's what he really wants. And maybe his behaviour and he'd settle down more. He wants to live with his father and although it would upset me I told him he could go, but his father said he's too much hard work, he wouldn't have him.

We asked families to what extent they had felt their problems to be within their control prior to referral to the child and family support service and how they felt by the time of the first interview. Most (83 per cent) had felt these problems to lie outside their control prior to contact with the child and family support services.

Since referral to the service, this percentage had dropped to just under half (49 per cent). Given that most families talked positively about the value of support it is probably encouraging and may indicate that the workers were indeed empowering the parents in this sense.

What the CFSS workers said

Workers generally shared families' views of the risk of accommodation at the point of referral. In 25 cases when parents had asked for their children to be accommodated they thought they had managed to avoid this. Similarly, they maintained seven children within their families, despite their requests for accommodation. More rarely, children were accommodated who did not wish to be (three children) or whose parents were against this course of action (seven). In these cases there was generally concern for the child's safety. At the point of referral to child and family support services, there is some evidence that staff were able to fulfil their brief to prevent out-of-home placement (but see also chapter 10). These endeavours did not always succeed, and six children were eventually accommodated at a later point.

We asked workers to estimate how much 'at risk of accommodation' they considered the target child in a referred family to be at two points in time:

■ at the point they were originally referred; and
■ at the time the interview was conducted, which was generally several weeks later.

Table 4.3 summarises their responses. Workers considered that level of risk had increased in 18 cases from the point of referral to the time of the interview. On the other hand, 10 cases had moved from being seen as 'high risk' to 'low risk', and a further 25 'high risk' cases were regarded as 'low risk' at the time of interview. These data are not easy to interpret and one can really only speculate as to the reasons underlying these shifts in perceived risk. The broader family preservation literature suggests that social workers' estimations of risk of imminent placement are generally not well honed, and this would appear to be case here (see Pecora and others, 1991)

There may also be other influences at work. This was one of the few therapeutic services to which field social workers could refer needy families, and the child and family support service was eager to help where it could. It may be that the criterion 'risk of imminent breakdown' was more frequently used than was justified for those cases which clearly did not meet other referral criteria such as school exclusion. This may be one factor in the apparent diminution of risk between referral and the

Table 4.3 Changes in workers' estimates of 'risk of accommodation'

		Risk of accommodation at interview					
		None	Low	Medium	High	Accommodated	TOTAL
Risk of accommodation at referral	None	1					1
	Low		29	1			30
	Medium		19	16			35
	High		10	25	17	6	58
	Accommodated			1	1	23	25
	TOTAL	1	58	43	18	29	149

time of interview, when families were in touch with the service. It is also the case that social workers may tend to overestimate the degree of diminution of risk for families with whom they are working. The increased risk for some families may be symptomatic of the fact that some threats to family life were not readily open to influence by the child and family support worker, for example, problems with an ex-partner or the influence of peers over a young person.

By the time of interview, the numbers of children in out-of-home placement had increased from 23 to 29. All six children were perceived as being at high risk of placement at the point of referral. The retrospective nature of these judgements, together with the general picture painted above, does not enable us to conclude that these six placements indicate an ability accurately to predict risk of imminent out-of-home placement.

5. Types of problems presented by children and families

As we have already seen in the previous chapter, the types of problems that children and families are bringing to the child and family support service are complex and wide-ranging. Many families have multiple problems. Here we examine in more detail the patterns and types of problems that children and families were bringing to the child and family support service, as reported by the child and family support staff.

The broad picture

Most problems were identified as existing at the point of referral, with relatively few emerging after that time with the exception of domestic violence (past and present) which was one problem that emerged after referral in 16 cases.

The overall picture suggests that child and family support staff were acting on the information accompanying the referral (see chapter 4). Given that staff are typically asked to undertake specific pieces of work in a time-limited period this is not unreasonable, assuming that a good quality assessment is there to act upon. However it seems unlikely that this was routinely the case. The criteria for referral to the service states that 'The importance of referrers undertaking a good quality initial assessment is emphasised'. The analysis of closed cases highlighted the paucity of assessment activity in the majority of cases (see chapter 7). The child and family support services themselves acknowledged the absence of this important step in the helping process, explaining that this had previously been seen as part of their job, until the reorganisation had introduced a short-term focus to their work.

Relationship problems

Problems between parents and children

By far the largest groupings of problems, according to workers, are relationship problems, particularly those between parents and children (mentioned 191 times). These problems were often long-standing, possibly stemming from early parenting and child management problems. This picture was also evident from the analysis of closed cases, where behaviour problems at both home and school were evident, together with more extreme forms of antisocial behaviour, delinquency and school exclusion. Such problems are related to, or exacerbated by, lack of knowledge of children's needs and an inability to manage adequately children's behaviour. These last concerns were raised 182 times by workers talking about the families on their current workloads.

Problems between adults

Relationship problems between adults were also long-established, and often took place across family units: parents who had separated or divorced, and whose ongoing conflicts continued to impact on the children and their relationship with their parents. In general, the service was expected to be able to address these problems in the context of short-term and not very intensive contact with families.

Violence

Interpersonal violence, both between parents, between parents and children and between young people/siblings were common features of these cases. Domestic violence and parental conflict were also a regular feature of the closed cases that we analysed.

> The largest grouping of problems were 'relationship problems' between parents and children and between adults, often across family units. Violence was a common feature of these cases. The problems were often long-standing and complex but the service was expected to address them with short-term interventions.

School related problems

Problems with school attendance and/or school exclusions feature as major sources of problems, reflecting the fact that this is an interdisciplinary service with a specific brief to prevent school exclusion as well as family breakdown. The combined evidence of this study (from closed cases, from our analysis of working agreements, and from interviews with parents) suggests that referrals are arriving too late for optimum chance of effective preventive work, either with regard to preventing the escalation of school problems leading to school exclusion or to the prevention of out-of-home placement (see chapter 10).

The evidence also raises the question whether one can tackle problems at school anywhere other than *in* the school. If one is trying to change behaviour, it is usually necessary to intervene either in the antecedent conditions that set the scene for, or 'trigger' behaviour, or in the consequences that follow that behaviour. It may be that an analysis of a child's misbehaviour at school, or his or her underachievement, would indicate that these are in part due to learning problems, an unappealing curriculum, or the inadvertent reinforcement of poor behaviour by staff or other pupils. Although one can bring about changes in such circumstances by persuading the individual to think and/or behave differently, and although sometimes the resolution of other problems (at home, for example) can make a difference, these are the exception rather than the rule. This is one reason why locating social workers and other helpers *in* schools, rather than outside them, merits serious consideration. Further, locating social workers in schools (rather than teachers in family centres) might go some way to de-stigmatising social work help, and enhancing its preventive capacity. Certainly, the prevalence of school exclusion and related problems evident in this and other studies (see Bagley and Pritchard, 1998), indicate the need for early effective intervention to prevent problems deteriorating to the point at which it disrupts the child's education, or that of his or her peers.

> The data underline the need for early intervention in cases when children's behaviour or school work show the first signs of deterioration, and for an evidence-based approach to policy and practice in this area. This also raises the question as to whether child and family support services might be more appropriately located within schools, rather than within social services.

Child abuse and neglect

Child abuse was specifically mentioned 52 times and neglect 17 times, although these are not priority groups for the service. Abuse and neglect were most frequently raised in the working agreements as tangential problems (such as concerns about physical punishment in the context of concerns about parenting adequacy overall). A small minority of cases involved the staff working to assess a parent's ability adequately to parent, or trying to bring about changes in order to prevent the out-of-home placement of a child for these reasons.

Health problems

Drug and alcohol abuse were less frequently mentioned than one might expect when comparing this group of families with those typically described as at 'imminent risk of breakdown' in the wider literature. This probably reflects the fact that most studies have been conducted in North America where drug and alcohol misuse have hitherto been more widespread than in the UK. The relatively low levels of reported mental health problems are also somewhat out of kilter with the general views of workers that mental health problems, particularly for young people, was an area that was under-resourced within the region, contributing to a number of inappropriate referrals. In this sample, workers regarded only two of the young people referred to them with mental health problems as inappropriate referrals.

Problems that workers did not highlight

Rather surprisingly, staff did not often cite problems with housing, debt or social isolation. When specifically prompted about these and other factors, the picture of a family's difficulties broadened considerably (see Table 5.1).

Why is this so? The differences require careful interpretation. Generally, inventories prompt people to consider things they might not otherwise consider. In other words, it is possible that the discrepancies are simply due to the differential responses routinely elicited by 'open-ended question' compared with those elicited by something akin to a 'multiple-choice questionnaire'. It is also the case that workers did not typically draw on a detailed written record or assessment when interviewed, and this may have led them to concentrate on more 'vivid' aspects of a family's difficulties. It may also be that the additional problems the workers

Table 5.1: Additional problems recognised by workers

Problem	Volunteered by workers (unprompted)	Recognised by workers (prompted)
Financial stressors	3	79
Housing stressors	10	48
Environmental problems	141[1]	12
Social isolation	6	67
Physical health problems	34	38
Mental health problems	26	60
Substance misuse problems	34	51
Care of dependants	0	22
Lack of co-operation from other agencies	0	57

1 Includes: lack of utilities, racism, conflict with neighbours

identified when specifically asked were not, in fact, central to the case. Like social workers more generally, it is also possible that child and family workers focus primarily on those areas they see themselves as able (or briefed) to do something about, and give less attention to problems beyond their immediate influence (see Macdonald, 2001).

It is possible that field workers were providing help with these other difficulties, but there was little evidence of this. In the absence of an adequate assessment, it is always possible that the course of action chosen will not be appropriate, or will only go some way towards tackling a family's problems.

Child and family support workers, like social workers more generally, focus primarily on those areas they see themselves as able (or briefed) to do something about, and give less attention to problems beyond their immediate influence, such as poverty. This selective bias may distort assessments, and in the absence of adequate assessment, may bias the selection of organisational responses.

6. The knowledge and values that informed the teams' approach

The child and family support staff who took part in our research combine the expertise of seasoned teachers and social workers (see chapter 3). We were interested to find out what motivated the staff in their work and what knowledge and values informed their decision-making. We also wanted to explore how this comparatively well-trained workforce were meeting some of the requirements of an 'evidence-based' approach to addressing the problems of children and families. The first part of this chapter is based on information provided by staff in background interviews conducted at the outset of the study, and on questionnaires they completed prior to interview.

The chapter also includes data from the interviews with families who told us what they thought of the way the workers approached them and their problems.

Reasons for working in child and family support

The teams were highly motivated and concerned with the quality of the service they provided. Although there were some problems, it is to their credit that they were largely supportive of this evaluation of their work even in a climate of cost-cutting.

Seven of the workers had previous experience in residential work and felt that this experience had shaped their understanding of why, where appropriate, preventing the accommodation of young people was so important. It had also contributed to their desire to work in a preventive way with children and their carers.

> I started work in social work and residential work many years ago and I thought there was something missing within residential and that was basically working collectively with the family and then when most of the [the large] residential units started to close down in the 70s – I had the opportunity to

work in one of these units – and then I could see the relevance and importance of a unit like this, how we'd actually work with parents and work with youngsters.

Five members of staff said they had chosen family centre work because field team social work provided few such opportunities for face-to-face work. They also described field social work as rather bureaucratic and intertwined with a child protection role which made it difficult, both logistically and therapeutically, to provide the help that families needed.

> I was always having to give children the message 'something more important than you has to be done urgently'. And in this job because you're not doing duty and you're not doing child protection investigations, you don't have to leave people high and dry ... you don't have to let people down all the time, which on district was a constant theme of really letting people down. Particularly letting down the vulnerable people we have responsibility for, namely the kids in care. Well it's like 'they're safe, they're in a children's home. It's not like they're being battered or neglected.' That's the bit that had to go out the window ... I hated that.

The teachers, whilst working as teachers in schools, had recognised the close inter-relationship between children's family circumstances and problems presented or experienced in school, and had sought opportunities to address these more adequately. This had entailed working with children with special needs and/or in therapeutic communities, and led ultimately to joining the child and family support service.

All the staff were committed to their work and clearly saw it as important, indeed as essential. They were highly aware of the need to provide a service oriented to the user.

Knowledge base

The child and family support workers were asked to identify any theoretical frameworks they found particularly pertinent or helpful to work with children and families, and to identify skills that they regarded as essential to this area of work. The reason for this was to explore the extent to which child and family support workers adopted an informed and reasoned approach to how they perceived the problems families presented, and to find out what informed their decisions about how best to help them. We were interested to explore this on the individual level and at the level of the team as a whole.

Not unusually, the first request presented some difficulty for a number of respondents, particularly in relation to the ways they conceptualised the problems that brought families into contact with the service (see Marsh and Triseliotis, 1996). Generally the response was that they, like most of their colleagues, were eclectic, drawing on a range of theories. That said, it was not easy to tease out what those theories were, or in what circumstances they would be used.

Where theoretical approaches were mentioned, systems theory (family therapy), learning theory (behaviour therapy and cognitive behaviour therapy), brief therapy and solution-focused approaches were mentioned most often. The latter approach was dictated by the felt pressure to work on a short-term basis, rather than any track record of effectiveness (see Davies, 2001, for brief accounts of these approaches).

Values and skills base

The child and family support workers were much clearer about the value base that informed their work, their general approach to families, and core skills. Workers were virtually unanimous in citing the importance of listening to families and to young people, and 'getting alongside them' (terminology which was a clear legacy from residential work for some), and to be able to do this quickly:

> I think there's the skill about, you know, listening to people and sort of acknowledging that they're doing the best they can while, at the same time, holding a bit of hope that you can change something ... and I think that – don't know whether that's a skill or an attribute really – there's something about holding a bit of hope for people.

> The analogy that I see for myself, I guess, has therapeutic origins, in that I actually believe that the reason I get to see them is because they are not used to having adults come alongside them and guide them to some other place, but that they are used to seeing adults as adversaries, largely.

Also embedded in these quotes is a view, frequently articulated, that it is important to see parents and children as trying to solve problems, and doing the best they can. In other words, adopting a positive and non-judgemental attitude whilst trying to help each party find ways, or perhaps better ways, of resolving their difficulties. Often this was talked about as 'empowerment' and contrasted with the negative experience of families that most families appeared to have had with education, social services and other helping bodies:

So I come in and listen, that's not just listening to the person, that's listening to the child as well. And from then on, it is empowering, because I think lots of the parents have actually been disempowered, no-one is listening, they've been through the education system, social system, etc. etc. [and no-one has listened]

Evidence-base for practice

One of the questions we put to all respondents was how the teams had determined the range of services they should provide. The question was designed to explore whether or not there was anything approaching a 'logical fit' between the way that the teams conceptualised the problems they dealt with, and the services they provided to tackle them.

Most respondents found this very difficult to answer. The majority gave a description of what was provided or had been provided. Some mentioned discussions that were taking place about future provision. What was missing in each case was any sense of why *these* approaches (such as group work, family therapy, counselling) were adopted. How were they thought to address the needs of families and young people? What was the evidence for their choices, either in terms of how they perceived problems or what they knew of the effectiveness of particular interventions?

It may be that workers felt these questions are settled. Family centres nationally provide a range of services, including group work, counselling, couples work, family work and direct work with children, and the social service department's own profile of CFSS services reflects this. But addressing the question of 'What kinds of group for what kinds of service users, with what kinds of problems?' is another and more challenging matter. For example, within the category of 'individual work' the department's profile of the work of the child and family support service refers to work focused on 'resolving personal, family and education difficulties'. It goes on to say, 'Methods may include task centred case work, counselling, and other approaches such as volunteer befriending, *depending on the identified needs of the child and her/his family* [our emphasis]'. One might argue that the phrase 'depending on the identified needs' indicates that staff are expected to select methods judiciously, but 'needs', despite its widespread use and popularity, is not a very helpful concept in this context.

What is required is a careful analysis of how problems have arisen, what is maintaining them, what we know about 'what works' (or might work) in such circumstances and *therefore,* what it might logically make sense to do (see Department of Health, 2000; Macdonald, 1998 and 2001; Macdonald and Sheldon, 1992).

Apart from family therapy, few units of work (groups, individuals, etc.) were described in terms of their therapeutic content or rationale, and there was only a limited sense of a strategic planning approach to case work.

It is important to stress that this is not an unusual state of affairs (see Marsh and Triseliotis, 1996). Social work training has encouraged workers to take a fairly uncritical approach to the selection of theory and to downplay the importance and critical appraisal of research – despite long-standing challenges to such an approach (see Sheldon, 1978). Only one respondent appeared fully to grasp this nettle.

> I think my biggest criticism really about the way the service is set up is that we set up with objectives and under current methods we don't have sort of a clear way of achieving these objectives. What I would like to see is our strategic planning sort of working with us … looking at different ways of working and actually say, right, the evidence suggests that this is a really effective way of working, let's train our staff and work through, rather than everyone doing sort of what they've done for years.

This reflection captures a critical challenge to the development of evidence-based practice. At present, there is little external pressure influencing the *content* of social workers' work other than their own personal experience or preferences, or their training histories. In contrast, the adoption of an evidence-based policy might well legislate *for* certain approaches and *against* others and as such, might be heavily resisted by social workers generally.

> Knowledge about what works with what sorts of problems, and in what circumstances, appeared not to be informing delivery on the ground. If it was, then workers found this hard to articulate. There is scope for a more 'logical fit' between the problems that families and young people are facing and the services provided to address these.

Differentiating between method and process

The quite proper emphasis on values and the importance of process in working with vulnerable and oppressed groups, has perhaps resulted in a tendency to see 'empowerment' almost as a *method* of work itself, rather than as a way of working or a goal. This may well be why some staff placed so much emphasis on empowerment as an operating principle. We argue that focusing exclusively on empowerment rather than tackling substantive issues about the content of services is no longer a tenable position.

The most effective intervention may well fail if delivered by someone who behaves in a dictatorial or cavalier fashion, or who lacks empathy, warmth and genuineness, or who does not work towards enabling users to enhance their problem-solving capacities. But if a problem is one of lack of knowledge or skill, or even a lack of resources, the *way in which we approach service users* will not compensate for poor choices in the *content of the service* we provide. Whilst there is considerable uncertainty about 'what works' or 'what works best' in certain circumstances, there are some areas where there is more evidence available to compare the relative merits of particular interventions with others. For example, behavioural and cognitive behavioural approaches are the intervention of choice for most behavioural problems and many emotional ones (see Kazdin and others, 1992).

> Empowerment is an important goal in social work with vulnerable and oppressed people. It is an important focus in the process of working but is not a method in and of itself. Empowerment may be an essential component of working sensitively and accountably with service users, but it cannot compensate for poor choices in the content of the service that is provided.

What families thought of child and family support workers

Families were generally positive about child and family support workers whom they generally saw as being in a different league from locality team social workers. This reflects a dominant theme throughout this study of a polarisation between the work that locality social workers and child and family support workers are able to do.

The differences were generally presented in terms of the apparent ability of child and family support workers to engage with families; to take seriously their problems and not to be judgemental. In technical terms, they scored well on empathy, warmth and genuineness (Truax and Carkhuff, 1967). As important, they were available, they returned calls and they did their best to help:

Respondent E: Well I don't think social services have been very good at all but [the CFSS worker] has been brilliant – she comes to visit and she's waiting ages – like two hours – we have meetings when we have all the family here we all say our little bit and whatever and I find that useful.

Respondent F: The social worker is negative, and [CFSW] is more positive.

Child and family support workers were seen to be reliable, as well as available, in contrast to locality team social workers who were often criticised for being unavailable, frequently (it seemed to families) on leave or off sick.

That said, families had some criticisms of the service. They would have liked the service to be available outside of office hours, and generally to be more readily available to families who needed help. The wish to be able to call on staff outside of office hours is in keeping with the approach to family preservation services found in the wider literature, where work is not confined to 9–5 or to weekdays only. In this sense, the service was perceived in the same way as social services more generally:

Q: How helpful have social services been overall?

A: I'll tell you what they haven't done if that helps! They are never there when you want them. I find the problem is that because I'm at work about half-past four or five o'clock there is no-one there and on Friday that's it for the weekend. There is no-one there. I just sit there and think, well what on earth can I do?

This is clearly a resource and organisational issue. Some families felt left in no doubt about the limited availability of child and family support staff:

Respondent G: They came back around 4.30 but really they were looking at their watches all the time because it was almost 5 o'clock, that's how I felt. I know we all have families, but when you take certain types of jobs ... if you were in an operating theatre, you can't look at your watch at 5 o'clock and go home, and I wasn't happy about that really.

Respondent H: ... nothing happened first of all because of holidays! – it was a terrible time – I mean we got allocated the worker who as far as I am aware only works three days a week, part time. What actually happened was she couldn't see me on one day and then she went on holiday for two weeks – my social worker was also on holiday at the same time and then she was sick for a week or so – and I just had no-one.

Comments like these suggest that for some families, a more flexible and responsive service is sometimes important. The only available source of help outside of office hours is the Duty and Assessment Team, but this is far removed from the family preservation concept of 24-hour, intensive service provision by one or two people (see, for example, Pecora and others, 1992; Schuerman and others, 1994; Schwartz and others, 1991).

There were exceptions. Some child and family support workers clearly appreciate these issues and go out of their way to maximise their availability in spite of organisational constraints:

> I felt they were actually very flexible and you know [family worker] saw us, like you know, 5.30 to 6.30 when most people weren't working ... Also, we've had review sessions at my house at about 5.30.

Families valued the service, found the workers easy to talk to and particularly appreciated their reliability and availability. Some families would like a more flexible and responsive service that is available outside office hours.

Child and family support in the wider context of social services

As we have seen, families made a clear distinction between the child and family support service and that provided by locality team social workers. They clearly prized the child and family support service. At the heart of this dilemma is the long-standing issue of 'care and control' or 'support and protection', with the child and family support service able to provide more of the first two with only minimal (though clearly stated) obligations in relation to the latter. But it is more than that. Field social workers are less able to engage in roles that would have been commonplace even ten years ago, namely providing help and assistance including, in some cases, the kinds of therapeutic help that the child and family support service aspires to provide. At the same time, they are gatekeepers to scarce resources such as the service in question here. It is an unenviable and stressful role. Service users often felt aggrieved at the lack of help they had received from locality team social workers and at not being referred to such a service earlier.

The role of social workers in providing this kind of therapeutic help is a contentious issue for some. As other professions have become more active in therapeutic service provision, their associated upward mobility has led some to question the competence or appropriateness of social workers participating in this work (even though social work led the way, and continues to do so in some areas). The pressure on social workers to perform their child protection and other legal duties to high standards has undoubtedly exacerbated this. The net result is that we see qualified social workers conducting a predominantly administrative function, acting as gatekeepers of scarce resources and referrers to others. Even advocacy is increasingly seen as something that should be located outside the social work profession. This can be very frustrating for the social worker, as we heard earlier from the child and family support worker who had previously been a field social worker:

> I was always having to give children the message 'something more important than you has to be done urgently'.

Whilst there is an important role for competent case management, there is no evidence to suggest that this function is best divorced from others, and indeed in child protection, the desirable attributes of case management (clarity, accountability, monitoring and review) are best located with the line-manager/supervisor (see Hess and others, 1992).

For most users of social services, unless there is a need for a very specialist service, it is highly likely that the social worker will be the only person in a position to offer any help at all. Given that it is increasingly unlikely that such help will be forthcoming from field workers, it is the more essential that it is available from social workers working in services such as child and family support. We would argue that, with appropriate training, social workers are in many circumstances best placed to offer such help, familiar as they are (and generally undaunted by) the range of problems that beset their service users.

Family support used to be part of what field social workers did. Increasingly this role is being relocated to specialist teams such as the one studied here. Such a segregation of tasks and responsibilities, combined with high thresholds of eligibility for either source of service provision, means there is a danger that families are unlikely to receive the help they need at the time they need it.

7. Assessments

In order to make appropriate decisions about how best to tackle particular problems, it is important to be knowledgeable about how such problems develop over time, what factors maintain them and what factors help to ease them, or to mitigate their consequences. This is particularly the case in social work, where the problems in question can be very complex indeed. Making sense of family discord or patterns of antisocial behaviour, and choosing a course of action most likely effectively to improve such situations, is challenging work. In order to make sensible decisions about how best to proceed, one needs a sound understanding of the problems with which one is dealing and one also needs to be able to select and implement those interventions known to be most effective in these circumstances. In other words, one not only needs to know 'what works' (in the sense of what kinds of interventions have the best record of success in similar situations) but one needs also to be able to tailor these to the particular circumstances of the families with whom one is working. Assessment is therefore an important component of an evidence-based approach to decision-making, and in this chapter we look at how assessments were carried out in our study area.

The fact that we found many ways in which practice could be improved is not an indictment of individual workers and their practice. It is more a reflection of the need for investment by social services departments and by those responsible for qualifying training.

Social workers all over the UK have been facing similar difficulties with completing adequate assessments and this is one reason why the Department of Health has since published the Framework for the Assessment of Children in Need (Department of Health, 2000). This research was carried out before this publication so we include a brief discussion to contextualise our findings within recent developments.

This discussion about assessments is mainly based on data gathered in our analysis of the closed files (see Appendices 1 and 3) but these findings were confirmed by other sources of data in this study. What follows encompasses the work of both locality team social workers and child and family support workers.

Assessment in the context of social work

Social workers are trained to regard assessment as an 'ongoing activity', and this approach is reiterated in the revised framework produced by the Department of Health (DoH, 2000). The problem with this approach is that assessment is often not regarded as a discrete task to be undertaken – an idea that *is* being corrected in the revised Department of Health guidance. As a result of this approach, public inquiries have frequently criticised social services departments (and others) for not having pieced together a family's history and current circumstances with the result that children have been left in dangerous situations, often with fatal results:

> Indeed throughout all our dealings with the family one can find nothing that could be recognised as a full or systematic assessment.
>
> Bridge Child Care Development Service, 1995

The absence of a recognisable assessment is not confined to child abuse inquiries (see, for example, Social Services Inspectorate, 1986 and 1994; Sanders and others, 1999; Macdonald, 2001).

What is assessment?

Without a good understanding of the development and nature of a problem it is unlikely that one will make sound decisions about interventions, whether those interventions are organisational, therapeutic or legal. This is clearly recognised in the social services department's criteria for referral to the child and family support service which states that 'The importance of referrers undertaking a good quality initial assessment is emphasised.'

Deciding what should count as an assessment was a much-discussed issue within the research team. The approach taken in this study was inclusive and sought to capture the different kinds of levels of assessment that social workers saw themselves as undertaking:

- To identify assessments within the closed files, whether explicitly labelled as such or not.

- To identify 'comprehensive assessments'. Comprehensive assessments are those assessments that followed the guidance offered by the Department of Health in 1988, now superseded by the revised framework (DoH, 2000).
- To identify what are typically called 'initial assessments'. Initial assessments are brief statements of the problems and what was thought to be needed based on early contact with the family. Initial assessments are often more accurately described as a screening exercise. However, sometimes they contained information that would have contributed to a 'proper assessment' and it was as much to ensure that we were not too rigid in our appraisal of this important area of activity that we recorded initial assessments.
- To evaluate the quality of assessments and/or assessment material according to certain criteria regarding scope, content, sources of information and the critical appraisal and use of that information. We asked a number of specific questions concerning the file, such as: 'Was there a social history?' 'Was there an account of how problems had developed and what was maintaining them?' 'Was there a problem formulation?'. Appendix 4 itemises all these questions. The files were 'interviewed' against this schedule but with a sympathetic 'interviewer'. We counted assessments irrespective of who had undertaken them.

Lack of assessment in the closed files

Our analysis of the closed files revealed a dearth of recognisable attempts at undertaking an assessment. Given that assessment is an analytic and reflective task, it is unlikely that the absence of assessments on files can be taken only to indicate an absence of a formal record. Indeed, it is difficult to conceive of one without the other. The case record is itself as much an assessment tool as a record of the process and its conclusions – or should be.

Initial assessments

In the most recent episode for all 152 service users, an initial assessment was identifiable in 64 per cent of cases. In a number of cases where no initial assessment was undertaken, this was probably because the referral episode was very brief (one day), and the referral was dealt with on the phone or by letter. However, this does not account for all of the cases and one might expect to find something that would have met our criteria of an initial assessment, given that it was very generous, in most if not all cases.

Full and comprehensive assessments

Full assessments were rare, and comprehensive assessments rarer still. For example, in the most recent episode (all 152 cases) only 29 per cent (43) files contained a full assessment, 24 of which were identified as *comprehensive assessments* (Department of Health, 1988). This pattern was replicated across referral episodes. Where they existed, assessments typically suffered from a number of weaknesses. In particular, assessments rarely:

- Contained a social history.
- Provided an account of how the families' problems had developed over time.
- Drew together information from a range of sources.
- Made explicit who had contributed to the assessment, where it had taken place, or how long it had taken.
- Contained any reference (explicit or implicit) to a theoretical framework or an empirical basis for the approach taken. Rarely was there any reference (explicit or implicit) to what is known about the development of problems.
- Made explicit the assumptions that workers brought to the assessment task, concerning why and how problems had developed or what it would therefore be appropriate to do. When 'implicit', such assumptions can constitute a major source of potential bias and therefore error. This is one reason why the active consideration of alternative explanations or alternative courses of action is very important in decision-making, and perhaps explains why alternatives were rarely considered in these files (see Macdonald, 2001).

Assessments of the nature of problems faced by children and families were not routinely happening. Assessments that were carried out were often marked by problems which undermined their quality and usefulness. These could be addressed in a number of ways. Some of these are addressed in the revised Department of Health assessment framework (DoH, 2000). This study identified: taking a social history; providing an account of the development of a family's problems and the factors which maintain them and/or prevent their resolution; drawing on information from a variety of sources, including other professionals; being explicit about how information is obtained and how it is evaluated; making clear the evidence base informing the work (both empirical and theoretical) and making explicit assumptions about how and why problems have developed, and how and why proposed plans are thought likely to help.

Does the 'Assessment Framework' address these problems?

There have been numerous attempts to improve the consistency and quality of information recorded on social work files. Generally, as inspection reports, inquiries and research all indicate, these have come to nothing. The authority in question was introducing another new system at the time this report was being compiled, and the Department of Health has since launched its initiative, aimed specifically at improving the incidence and quality of assessments. It may well improve the former. We are somewhat sceptical of the likelihood that, on its own, this will bring about significant improvements in the quality of the assessments produced. There are many reasons for this, and these are summarised below. Most significant is the fact that telling people *what* information to collect does not enable them critically to appraise it, to make sense of it, or to recognise its significance. Assessment is a skilled activity, inextricably linked to the knowledge base that informs it. The new framework provides pointers to what it considers to be important knowledge in making good assessments, but in and of itself it cannot address the gaps in people's knowledge, or in their assessment *skills*.

Bearing in mind that *some* of the problems we identified might have been, in part, attributable to pressures on staff which resulted in them not recording their views adequately in the file, it seems that the changes required to improve this area of practice straddle resources, management and skills. In addition to the useful structure provided by the Department of Health's assessment framework, a number of other changes are needed:

Conditions for improving assessment in practice

■ **Time to do it**

Recording is a time-consuming activity and for staff who are beset by more tasks than they can reasonably be expected to manage (or to manage well), recording inevitably takes a back seat, except for the most conscientious of practitioners.

■ **Practical support**

Staff in this local authority had poor administrative backup (in terms of quantity) and minimal access to Information Technology. Staff need the back-up and the skills to use it.

■ **Clear departmental guidance about priorities**

Clear instructions are needed as to what can be left *undone*. A general operating principle tends to apply to recording in general, namely: 'you decide what you leave until tomorrow and when something goes wrong then we'll tell you your priorities were misguided' (see Macdonald, 1990).

■ **Opportunities for practising and developing skills**

Assessment, case planning, monitoring and evaluation are skilled activities. No framework, however appropriate, can compensate for an absence of skill in this area. Social work courses and further professional development need to equip their students with these skills. There is relatively little written on this subject within the social work literature (see Macdonald, 2001) and there is a need for more research-based information and guidance.

> Making assessments is more than gathering information; it is a skilled activity. This research suggests a number of conditions that managers need to consider if practitioners are to be able to improve their practice.

Plans for intervention

There was a clear plan of action attached to most of the assessments undertaken. On only two occasions, however, was reference made to effectiveness research. In other words, what we know about the effectiveness of a proposed course of action, and alternative courses of action was never recorded. Reasons were generally provided for the proposed plan but only in ten cases was it evident that these reasons had been shared with the parents and only in four cases with the child(ren). It is possible that this is an artefact of the record, but the absence of the child's voice within the file was striking, and this was but one reflection of this.

Were families clear about the assessment?

When we interviewed families who were currently receiving a service, there was some confusion about assessment that mirrored what we found in the closed cases.

More than a half of the parents did not know whether an assessment had been done or not. When families talked about assessments, it was clear that in many cases the families were referring to the working agreements or the periodic reviews of work, indeed anything that had been committed to paper. Despite the confusion about assessment, 40 per cent of parents thought the child and family support worker shared their view of where the problem(s) lay and another 13 per cent thought they shared some views.

I'd say [the child and family support worker] was the only one we'd come into contact with really and he was brilliant, he was the sort of chap you could sort of open up to and I found that talking to him, sometimes when you're having problems you question yourself and think you're a bad parent or what-have-you and although you know you're not, its nice to just be able to talk to someone and just get that little bit of support especially when you're feeling a complete failure yourself you know.

One third either did not know what the worker thought, or thought there was a difference of opinion about their problems.

> Only rarely were assessments in this study shared with parents and hardly ever with the child or young person. Families were mostly unclear about whether or not an assessment was being undertaken and if so by whom. They often thought the child and family support service were doing an assessment when, in fact, they were not. This has clear implications for the accountability of the service to its users.

Whose responsibility?

It appears then, that assessment is an area that would repay investment. In this study, there was no identifiable link between the services provided and a careful assessment of a family's difficulty. For the most part, families did not know whether or not an assessment had been done, and could not shed light on how they thought the workers conceptualised their difficulties, although a number thought the worker shared their view of 'where' the problem lay, e.g. with the young person. The child and family support staff recognised this problem. In the past they had seen this as part of their role, but now regarded it as that of the locality social worker, unless the referral was specifically for assessment – which was not often. The locality social workers appeared to be reaching decisions about the need for support in a general sense (effectively making a judgement about the threshold level of need for referral to the service) but without the detailed assessment work that could direct the child and family support workers' endeavours. In other words, assessment was falling through the organisational hole resulting from the split between the child and family support service and their colleagues in locality teams.

8. Agreeing goals and action plans

The ability to set clear goals, and to identify specific outcome indicators that show that goals have been achieved, are central to monitoring and evaluation. Our research explored how goals were set and shared with children and families. We analysed working agreements, reviews and closing summaries of cases referred to the service and interviewed social workers (for further detail about methodology, see the appendices). We also explored how families understood the goals of the work.

The first meeting with families

On receiving a referral the child and family support staff set up a planning meeting with the family.

Who was at the meeting?

Most meetings were between the parents and the family support workers. Social workers were present on 60 per cent of occasions and the CFSS teachers at 10 per cent of meetings. We were told that few meetings start with a joint appraisal by social workers and teachers. Given the high number of school-related reasons for referral, this is perhaps surprising. When this was discussed with staff, they argued that often school-related needs became apparent in the course of the first meeting or some time after. However, this does not really accord with the number of times that school-exclusion features as a recorded reason for referral.

Families did not really know who had decided who should attend this meeting, but most (67 per cent) thought they understood why those who were there had been asked to attend and most thought they were appropriate (63 per cent).

According to parents, more than half of young people (53 per cent) were absent from meetings. An analysis of the records of planning meetings confirms this. We do not know why this was the case but the majority of families (75 per cent) were invited to meetings scheduled during the day-time (when young people were supposed to be at school). Only four per cent of meetings took place in the evening. In just over 15 per cent of cases no meeting was held, such as when a family was re-referred or circumstances precluded a meeting.

The purpose of the meeting

In the first meeting with families, workers aim to explain the service and what it could offer, explore with families their thoughts and feelings about the referral, identify what each participant sees as a problem and agree a plan of action. This session culminates in the completion of a working agreement which all parties sign, and which provides scope for registering dissent. This then forms the basis for a review of progress in a majority of cases, and an evaluation of work at the close of service.

Were the aims of the meetings achieved?

When interviewed shortly after their first session(s), workers described most of the families as 'co-operative' or 'generally co-operative', but a substantial minority as difficult to engage or even 'hostile'. A similar pattern was noted with young people themselves, though only two were described as 'hostile'. Workers were generally satisfied that their first meetings with families achieved their aims with a few exceptions. These included the refusal of a young person to participate or attend the meeting, or (in a small minority of cases) failure to establish a consensus about the nature of the problems and/or the changes which needed to be achieved.

Interviews with service users confirmed the view of workers that they were generally receptive to the child and family support workers:

> I don't know – I think the social workers just class you as anybody – she prob-
> ably says the same thing to me that she says to everybody – it is not personal
> – not even a little bit – so she is sat there and talks whereas with [child and
> family support worker] you – it is just totally different – you know you can tell
> him anything – I mean I have cried in front of him hundreds of times – just
> because of how depressed I have been – with her I don't tell her – I pretend

I am alright and say 'yes everything is fine' – but it isn't – but I will say to her 'everything is alright thanks'. She makes you feel like you can't be yourself – you can't tell her the really personal things – I just can't tell her.

[Parent 1] Yes they [the child and family support workers] are brilliant.
[Parent 2] They are really good.
[Parent 1] It is the only people we haven't moaned about isn't it?
[Parent 2] They feel safe to talk to.
[Parent 1] That was since she told us about the case conference, when she stuck up for us, and that stuck in my mind.

Nearly all families said they were made to feel welcome at this important meeting, and most said the purpose of the meeting was explained to them. Just over half the parents interviewed said they felt they had had an opportunity to talk about things that mattered to them (58 per cent) and most of these said they thought they had been taken seriously. A few parents said the meeting made them feel as if they were being blamed (mothers in particular – 13 per cent) and some said they felt protective of their child (9 per cent). One fifth of mothers said they felt angry and a further quarter said they felt frustrated. Almost half of parents said they felt listened to, either singly or jointly, and almost half felt relieved or supported.

> The way in which the first meetings with families were conducted suggests good practice. Families felt they were listened to and taken seriously and workers thought that for most families, the aims of the meeting were achieved.

Working agreements

As explained previously, the working agreement is summarised in a written record, designed to be signed by all parties.

The working agreement covers:

- what needs to change
- who is seeking the changes
- what the purpose of the work is
- what the desired outcomes are
- whether or not there is any disagreement between the parties
- what the action plan is.

Few of these records indicated disagreements between the people present at the meeting. Where disagreement was recorded this usually registered the refusal of the young person to participate. However, few of these agreements in fact included the child's view in an easily identifiable way (17 per cent) and, in 36 per cent of the agreements, this box was not completed (with the implication that there were no disagreements). Almost no agreements were signed by young people (just under 10 per cent) and only a quarter were signed by parents.

Goal setting

Clear goals are an important feature of evidence-based practice. Being clear and specific about what it is one is seeking to achieve provides both families and workers with a yardstick against which to assess progress.

Vague and non-specific goals

In response to headings on the forms, staff often did not distinguish between the overall 'purpose of the work', and 'desirable outcomes'. Under 'purpose of work' and 'desirable outcomes' some staff recorded very general (but definitely measurable) aims such as 'preventing accommodation' or 'preventing family breakdown'. Others were in some sense more specific but tended to record desired outcomes that were less easily observable, such as 'improving the atmosphere in the family'. In many cases, there was little qualitative distinction to be made between the stated purpose of the work and the outcomes that were identified as desirable.

Such general and non-specific goals are not useful for monitoring and evaluation or for accountability to service users. Here are some examples:

- [Parent] would like to see a change in the children's attitude.
- [Child's] behaviour needs to be modified both at home and at school.
- [Parent]to feel more in control of her reactions and of [child's] behaviour. Conflict between [parent and child] which could be risky.
  [Child's] confusion and anger.

Unless 'pinned down' to specific changes these are almost impossible to monitor. For example, anything *could* be described as a 'change in the children's attitude'. Similarly, feeling 'more in control' is difficult to ascertain, but more importantly *feeling* more in control does not necessarily mean that one *is*, although it might be important in its own right.

Some changes identified by workers were not really changes at all, but formulations or summaries of the problem, such as 'Mr and Mrs P say they find G's behaviour challenging'. Sometimes it is clear who needs to change (in these cases it is usually the young person's behaviour) but in only a minority do the records indicate in whose opinion these changes need to occur. When such forms are unsigned it is difficult to know whether the list of changes needed reflects the views of family members or workers, or both.

Good practice

Some agreements were exemplary in the specificity of the changes they identify as needing to take place.

■ For [child] to return home.
■ For [child] to carry out some chores in the house.
■ [Parents] to have better control of their bills and finances. For [father] not to swear and shout at the children but be able to talk to them. For [parents] to spend more social time with the children, going out to visit places, family and friends. [Parents'] communication to be clearer and better. [Parents] need to agree and make joint decisions regarding the children. The children's behaviour in terms of the way they act and talk with each other.

The last quotation addresses a number of changes that were identified as necessary in a family at risk of breakdown. Although there is still room for further clarity (for example, what will 'better control of finances' look like for *this* couple?) it is nonetheless very appropriate for an agreement formed at an early stage. It potentially provides a template against which to measure progress, and certainly is the basis of identifying useful outcome indicators (see chapter 10).

Was information located elsewhere?

Staff argued that because these forms had often to be completed in the limits of one meeting and were written with the family in mind, they often avoided 'technical' language and sometimes did not address difficult issues 'head on'. They pointed out that additional recording would provide a more detailed and accurate picture. However, where we had access to all recorded material (such as closed cases and some cases on file where working agreements were not available), this did not yield appreciably more information. Further, the working agreements, reviews and closing summaries that we examined have been interpreted in the context of information from other sources, including interviews with staff and families and data from the analysis of closed cases. No source provided evidence that what we found in the working agreements was not typical of the work as a whole.

> Examples of good practice in goal setting described changes that needed to take place in clear and simple language. They indicated *in whose opinion* these changes should occur and described desired outcomes that were observable and specific.

Sharing information with families

At the time of interview, even though for many families this was some time into the work with the child and family support service, one third said they had no idea about the proposed length of contact, and a further 20 per cent thought that their contact would be 'as long as necessary'. This is unexpected given the time-limited and contractual nature of the work of the service. It is recognised as 'good practice' for workers to give copies of the agreements to families. Families sign the contract, and a copy is sent to them. Delays in this sometimes relate to a lack of administration support in centres but it was not clear from the records whether or not this was routinely done. Only a small number of families referred to this information and even then had not absorbed the content properly. Almost half the families were expecting weekly contact of about one hour with CFSS. Most other families were not sure what to expect.

This study, along with a number of previous studies, highlights the fact that families have relatively little grasp of what it is that the workers are trying to achieve, or how they are trying to achieve it (see Rees and Wallace, 1982). Some staff, on consideration of an early draft of this report, made the point that sometimes their lack of clarity or specificity in their record was deliberate, particularly when these documents were open to parents, such as working agreements. The argument was made that sometimes, if the hunch is that a child is being abused, then being up-front about the purpose of sessions with a young person was counter-productive. They also pointed out that the agreement is the outcome of one or possibly two meetings and has to be framed in a user-friendly way. We understand this, but think that even in these circumstances there is scope for increased specificity, for example, 'I want to see (child) for six sessions in order to get to know him or her better, and try to find out why he or she is behaving like this'. Seeking clarity and specificity is an important step in helping families identify their concerns and set out what changes they are seeking.

Action plans

Most action plans comprised solely who was going to see whom, for how many sessions. Rarely, if ever, was there an indication of what was to be done in these sessions or how it was thought that this would achieve the purpose of the work or secure the desired outcomes.

Staff told us that there was no expectation placed on them to address the 'how' or 'why' aspects of work plans and the forms they used reflected this to some extent. Not surprisingly, then, staff felt the picture we painted did not do them justice in terms of their approach, and it is possible that the challenge was not in providing an informed plan of action, but in articulating it. Unfortunately, the only data we have are from written records and interviews, and both sources point to a problem in this area. It was not easy, in interviews, to elicit explanations of why a particular plan had been adopted, or how it was thought to achieve the aims and objectives. That said, a minority of staff were able routinely to anchor their plans in a theoretical or empirical framework.

How clear were families about the plan of action?

Just over one third of families said they were clear what the plan of action was (37 per cent), although this typically reflected a focus on who was spending time with whom, rather than on what was being done and why. For example:

> I think she was pretty good she could see the kind of problems and could see what was happening. She took [the young person] off a couple of times. [Plan of action?] That she would see [young person] on her own and take her off and do things with her. There were only about two times but it stopped because she [the worker] moved. More were planned but she moved.

A further one third were 'somewhat clear' (33 per cent), for example:

> She agreed with me that I needed the break and that pleased me to think that somebody's on my side. She agreed that she could see John's got problems and she could also see that he would feel being rejected again by his mum by not turning up at the meeting. I think she's seen quite a bit, there again she didn't say what she really seen to me but I can just presume what, what I think she seen.

The remainder were not at all clear, for example:

> I don't know what their proposals are now. None of it ever made any sense to me, like I said, because I haven't heard nothing now whether they're thinking well, because I've got the place in [name] School now anyway, whether they're just going to wait until next term and see what happens if he gets on at school, I don't know.

As with assessments, families were unclear about the working agreements and action plans. They often did not know what the workers were trying to achieve or how they were trying to achieve it. Working agreements could be improved by ensuring the clarity and specificity of goals and providing a clear rationale for a chosen programme of work that is agreed and understood by all participants.

9. The service response and expectations of success

Child and family support workers in this study area provide a more restricted set of services than those most often described in the family preservation literature. In the USA, family preservation services are often home-based, intensive and multi-focal, covering not only the provision of therapeutic services, but financial assistance and concrete help such as transport, advocacy, referral to other agencies and so on (see, for example, Feldman, 1991a; Rzepnicki and others, 1997; Schuerman and others, 1994).

The child and family support staff working for this social services department are only able to offer short-term, time-limited help of a not very intensive nature predominantly based in the family centres. The help that *is* provided focuses mainly on what might broadly be described as therapeutic interventions. Given that there is now considerable doubt in the literature about the effectiveness of even intensive, short-term family preservation services to prevent out-of-home placement, this may have implications for the likely effectiveness of this particular service. It may also account for the cautious optimism expressed by staff and families about the likelihood of achieving goals in such a short space of time. Families come to this service with problems that have a long and difficult history and, in a later discussion (chapter 11) we explore further the question of whether earlier help might improve outcomes.

Since the reorganisation of the child and family support service (see chapter 3) all of the families referred to the CFSS had a locality team social worker who was responsible for other areas of work such as assistance with practical problems and advocacy. Families' views about the adequacy of the services they did or did not receive from social services as a whole has some bearing on this discussion (see the discussions in chapters 6 and 11).

Most of the data in this chapter are based on interviews with staff and service users. We had hoped that analysis of the closed files would give us a more complete picture of service responses but, for reasons outlined in Appendix 3, this proved not to be the case.

Aims and content of work with families

Staff worked in a number of ways with families, sometimes seeing young people alone, sometimes seeing parents as a couple (or alone if a single parent) and sometimes working with the entire family, or those family members who would meet with them. Some teams also provided groups for young people and parents. These options were not mutually exclusive and families might receive more than one. Sessions were typically offered in packages of six, often at weekly or fortnightly intervals, with sessions varying from a half hour (generally with a young person) to an hour (with a couple or a family).

Work with parents

Workers were not overly optimistic about their abilities to achieve the goals they had agreed with parents, particularly regarding improving parents' understanding their child's needs. Table 9.1 summarises what workers said were their main aims in working with parents, and how optimistic they were about achieving these. 'Mostly'

Table 9.1 Optimism about achieving aims in sessions with parents

	Worker optimism about main aim			
Main aim of sessions	Completely	Mostly	Not at all	Total
Help communication between parents	–	–	2	2
Help parents work together	6	5	4	15
Improve parenting skills	3	4	2	9
Improve parents' understanding of child's needs	1	4	7	12
Boundary work	3	1	1	5
Advocacy	2	1	–	3
Building self-esteem / support	12	6	4	22
Identifying parents' needs	1	1	–	2
Working on parents' relationship	1	–	1	2
Child protection work	–	2	3	5
Assessment	3	–	3	6
Counselling	–	–	1	1
Not identified	1	–	–	1
TOTAL	33	24	28	85

optimistic is rather vague, but perhaps reflects the range of factors over which the workers had relatively little control such as the school or the peer group. They are most confident about tackling issues such as 'building self-esteem' or 'supporting parents' but such aims are amongst the least specific and, in the absence of clear outcome indicators (such as what improved self esteem would look like for *this* parent) are the most difficult to evaluate.

Workers also indicated a number of secondary aims in their work with parents. Most often mentioned were 'improvement of parenting skills' and 'parental under-standing of a child's needs' (11 mentions each) followed by 'building self-esteem/ offering support', 'boundary work' and 'advocacy' (7, 6, and 5 mentions respectively). A similar pattern emerged in relation to levels of optimism regarding the achievement of secondary aims.

Work with young people

A broadly similar pattern emerges when one considers the responses given by work-ers in relation to their aims and levels of optimism regarding their individual work with young people (see Table 9.2)

The most frequently stated aim is to 'give support and space to talk' and a number of others are related to this, such as 'engage' and 'build self-esteem' and again, staff were generally optimistic about achieving such non-specific aims. The general picture was replicated in relation to secondary aims where staff identified 'advocacy re school' on 17 occasions, 'support' and 'space to talk' and 'work to improve rela-tionships between young person and carers' on 13 occasions each. Aims of 'improve general behaviour' and 'build self-esteem' were each mentioned six times. Most other items were mentioned only once. Overall, workers were more optimistic still about achieving these secondary aims, with only six workers expressing misgivings about the likelihood of any success. Again, it is *areas of work*, rather than *aims* that appear most frequently, and perhaps accounts for the optimism that this can be achieved. In other words, it is the *process* that is the subject of optimism, rather than any particular outcome.

Work with families

Work with families was more specifically targeted at improving relationships between young persons and their carers and improving general communication. Twenty-one

Table 9.2 Optimism about achieving aims regarding sessions with young people

Main aim	Worker optimism about main aim			
	Completely	Mostly	Not at all	Total
Improve relationship between young person and parents	2	5	1	8
Improve relationship with siblings	–	1	–	1
Advocacy re school	4	5	0	9
Build self-esteem	2	5	1	8
Give support / space to talk	12	13	4	29
Anger management	–	–	1	1
Working with issues of risk / safety	3	5	1	9
Advocacy re youth justice	–	1	–	1
Risk assessment	2	2	1	5
Improve general behaviour	2	1	1	4
Practical help	2	–	1	3
To engage	3	1	2	6
Race identity work	1	1	0	2
Boundaries	0	1	1	2
Counselling	–	–	1	1
TOTAL	35	41	16	*93

other aims were mentioned, each only once. Focusing on these aims, workers were mainly optimistic about their chances of securing positive outcomes in their work with families.

> Workers were generally confident about achieving non-specific aims such as 'improving self-esteem' and 'providing support'. These aims, however, were rarely tied down to specific outcomes. Workers expressed less optimism about achieving other, more specific, aims. Although providing support and a place to be listened to and understood are essential ingredients of a child and family support service, this finding raises the question whether they are sufficient to achieve the overall aims of the service.

Does the service 'fit' the problem?

Overall, the content of work could be improved in relation to its evidence-base. Some staff had particular expertise in family therapy and others had some expertise in cognitive-behavioural approaches. Both show up reasonably well in outcome research, although the latter generally enjoy much more support (in terms of number and range of studies) than the former. Given the high incidence of behavioural and relationship problems, the choice of individual sessions with a young person is open to question, as is the emphasis on verbal influence through counselling (both of young people and their families). The history of outcome research in social work suggests that talk therapies are unlikely to be sufficient to secure behavioural or even attitudinal change (Rachman and Wilson, 1980; Fischer, 1973; Reid and Hanrahan, 1981; Macdonald and Sheldon, 1992; Reid, 1994). Whilst there is certainly scope for helping young people to articulate their problems with a view to helping them identify strategies for changing behaviour (whether their own or that of others) the weight of evidence is not in favour of this as a *sufficient* strategy. Approaches that focus on helping young people and their families to develop the skills necessary for problem-solving and developing and maintaining alternative ways of behaving are also required (see, for example, Rutter and others, 1998).

Behavioural approaches typically require an intensive short-term application, preferably in the settings where the behaviour occurs. They usually entail an active approach to their implementation rather than a 'counselling' format. There was little evidence that staff had the opportunity to use such approaches systematically or in a form that would maximise the chances of a good outcome.

> Work with families and young people showed a reliance on verbal forms of influence. Important as these are, research suggests these will rarely be sufficient to secure effective outcomes. An appropriate repertoire of interventions needs to be considered at a strategic and policy level for teams like these, in the light of research evidence of effectiveness.

What the families expected from the service

From the perspective of many families, referral to the child and family support service represented a long-awaited chance to tackle their difficulties. Most were referred to the CFSS by their social worker (63 per cent), a further 17 per cent being referred via the duty and assessment team, following a crisis. In other words, some 79 per cent of referrals were internal to social services.

Perhaps not surprisingly, given their experience prior to referral, just under a quarter of mothers (24 per cent) said they were optimistic that the service would be helpful. A further 29 per cent did not know, or were reserving judgement. One fifth of mothers were not at all optimistic. Taken in conjunction with the rather limited optimism expressed by workers in general, this is not the best foundation for effective work (see Bandura, 1977). Those fathers who were interviewed responded similarly.

One third of families had some prior knowledge of the family centres to which they were referred, two-thirds from previous experience and the remainder from other service users. Most of these families were pleased to be put back in touch with the service, either as the result of the re-emergence (usually) of problems with the referred child, or having been referred in respect of another child (indeed, some of the names of families interviewed or referred to the service in the study period also appeared in the analysis of cases closed to the service (at an earlier point). Just over half the families (54 per cent) had no clear idea of what to expect from the family centre staff. Only 28 per cent said they had been told something of what to expect by their social worker.

How did families think the CFSS might help them?

When asked for their views, half the parents we interviewed saw the purpose of the contact with CFSS as providing an opportunity for them to talk about problems, reflecting the emphasis that the workers themselves placed on this, and the frequency with which it appeared in the purpose of work recorded on the working agreements. Of those parents who talked about more outcome-oriented actions, 17 per cent thought it provided an opportunity to learn about new ways of dealing with the referred child and 14 per cent talked explicitly about improving parenting skills.

Related to this, 30 per cent of parents talked about improving the child's behaviour at school and 24 per cent about improving his or her behaviour at home. Eight parents (11 per cent) referred specifically to anger management and 13 per cent to securing access to other services. Sixty per cent of parents saw the contact with CFSS as providing an opportunity for the young person to talk – but the reluctance of some young people to engage with workers led to disappointment and frustration for some parents.

Did families believe the proposals were realistic?

Less than one fifth of families were clear that the proposals for action were realistic (18 per cent). Just under one fifth of parents considered the proposals unrealistic, and just over a quarter said they did not know. The remaining 15 per cent thought the proposals 'somewhat realistic'. When asked about their concerns a number of anticipated problems were cited as reasons why proposals might not come to fruition. Thirty per cent of families thought the young person would be unwilling to co-operate and a further 15 per cent said an important parent figure would be similarly unwilling. Child care, transport, work and timing of interviews were each mentioned by between two and five families. These factors perhaps account for the low levels of optimism that parents expressed about the likelihood that their problems would be resolved.

What did the children and young people think?

Of the 19 young people interviewed, only one said they thought they had an opportunity to talk about things that mattered to them, although two others said they felt they were taken seriously. Most referrals appeared not to have been made at the behest of the young people themselves, despite the fact that 60 per cent of parents said they hoped that the service would provide the young person with an opportunity to talk about things. It is not therefore surprising that a concern commonly voiced by parents was that young people did not want to participate in family sessions, or in individual sessions with workers. This was particularly frustrating for parents who so often saw the problems as lying 'within' or 'with' the child.

> *Respondent I:* [young person] went to see this particular worker and he is supposed to go and see her but he just refuses to go. He doesn't go down there so me and [his father] go down there just for a chat, but it was pretty pointless really if [young person] refuses to take any help, so we kind of dropped it off, and stopped going.

> *Respondent J:* When he [family worker] came to the house to visit [young person] he just walked out, didn't want to know at all.

In these circumstances, workers often switched their focus from sessions with the young person or with the family to sessions with parents, where the aim was to support them (as opposed to help in other, more specific areas such as couples counselling or parenting skills). In other words, workers not unreasonably focus their efforts on those who are 'available for influence'. Sometimes this is appropriate: parents can be mediators of change, for example. However, sometimes parents regarded this as inappropriate, if not pointless, when the problem, as they saw it, clearly belonged 'elsewhere'. Some parents rather resented it:

> Most time when she's been here, he's like been out there, or he's gone upstairs and he's like, haven't even been included in it. It always seems to be me that they're focusing on, and I thought originally the work was supposed to be done between the young person and my husband, not me, because it's their relationship.

Families and young people were not very optimistic about the prospects for change, which is perhaps not surprising given their history prior to referral. A common concern was the difficulty of encouraging young people to participate in sessions.

The need for a 'joined-up' approach to family support

The child and family support service does not exist in a vacuum. As well as receiving referrals from multiple agencies, the social services department (as well as families themselves) also tries to secure services from other agencies, particularly health and education. This reflects the multiple needs that most families experience. Organisational boundaries and resource shortages can exacerbate differences about the division of labour between agencies. Service users often fall through the gaps that open up in these boundary disputes or grey areas.

One example of this is that young people with mental health problems are sometimes dealt with by child and family support services because mental health services do not regard them as meeting their (rather high) threshold criteria, or simply because they do not have the capacity to provide a service. In these circumstances, child and family support services are used as a 'temporary support' to families waiting other, more appropriate forms of help. They also lobby on behalf of families to secure those services and/or secure them more quickly, and this is clearly appreciated. Here is someone whose child and family support worker has helped to secure psychiatric help for their son:

In the last week really – and it is probably psychiatric – they have arranged to get this order which apparently [CFSS worker] told me yesterday will open a lot of other avenues so hopefully now something is going to happen. [Interviewer: Workers are contacting other services?] Yes – it seems without their go ahead these services are impossible to access.

It is important that this context of 'stretch and make-do' is considered when we assess the work and outcomes of the child and family support services because, as the title of this report suggests, the child and family support workers are providing a much-needed service against the odds.

10. Outcomes

Mapping outcomes inevitably proved a difficult task for reasons that have already been discussed but which we briefly summarise here.

- **The lack of outcome indicators**

  Workers commonly confused *process* with *outcome* in the way in which they stated their aims (see chapters 7 to 9). In other words, they tended to describe what they planned *to do*, rather than whether particular *end-states* would be brought about. The aim might be, for example, *'To offer family sessions to address issues about family breakdown and enable family to find and implement solutions.'* As a goal, it does not specify any change or indicators that can be monitored, so it can be said to be 'achieved' simply by carrying out the sessions, regardless of whether or not an improvement is experienced by the family. An appropriately formulated outcome goal would specify exactly what changes it was hoped to bring about, providing concrete and unambiguous examples of how such changes would manifest themselves.

- **The limited scope of goals**

  A further problem, also discussed earlier (see chapter 5), was that goals tended to focus on fairly limited areas, rather than addressing the range of needs presented by families. This perhaps reflects the workers' tendency to work on areas where they felt they could have some influence, and which reflected the stated reasons why families were referred to them. This limited focus may have been a contributory factor in their limited optimism about bringing about change, particularly in the context of short-term intervention (chapter 9).

- **The complexity of problems presented**

  The main aims of the service are to prevent family breakdown and prevent school exclusion but these are very difficult to achieve (see chapter 2). Families using the service have complex and long-term problems (see chapters 4 and 5), some of which lie outside the remit of the child and family support service.

Given these difficulties in identifying outcomes, we have tried to piece together a coherent picture from various sources here using:

- data from interviews with the 72 families, of which 30 families were interviewed both shortly after receiving a service from the child and family support services and after the work had been completed;
- departmental management information, such as the number of children placed following case closure (to CFSS); and
- data from closing summaries.

Confirming data are referred to from the analysis of the closed files.

Amount of contact with the CFSS

Half the 30 families we interviewed could not say how many contacts they had had with the service. Of those that could remember, most said they had had between four and eight sessions. Data from the closing summaries suggest that this amount of contact was typical, although many families received substantially more and some substantially less. Eight families recalled they had missed sessions, some due to illness (1), due to working (1), due to being on holiday (3), or for reasons they could not recall (3). Eight families reported that sessions had been missed because the worker had cancelled them, largely for reasons they were unaware of.

Reviews and closing summaries often stated that planned sessions had not happened, or that only one or two meetings had taken place of those planned. The number of completed sessions was generally higher amongst those families we interviewed on two occasions, perhaps reflecting a higher level of willingness to engage, both with child and family support staff and with researchers. The pattern of contacts (with sessions offered to young people and to parents) was broadly similar to the sample as a whole.

Families' views of the services provided

Parents, like workers, often recognised the importance of being listened to and given an opportunity to talk things through. Some families commented on the constructive advice they had been given, particular in relation to managing difficult behaviour:

> I feel personally more hopeful now than I did before I met [child and family support workers] – because there are things that they actually come out with which maybe we were aware of but we didn't take seriously – like for instance

– when you say that you have got to mean it – we have known that for a long time but when it is explained to you and when we have done it we have seen the result. We bought a computer a while ago … [young person] played up that day and I wouldn't let him have a go and he begged – I am so sorry – there was a result – you know he apologised and I can see some light at the end of the tunnel at the moment whereas before there was none.

Others were less certain of the value of the services on offer, and some were frankly hostile:

Respondent K: We've been doing … we've been play acting silly arguments we've had but she just thinks it's funny, she sits and swears a lot.

Respondent L: We get in there and we have to do … the last time we went we had to do behaviour, attitudes and things, and they were doing aggressive behaviour, assertive behaviour and passive behaviour. And then you had a sheet with all these different things and you had to circle it to see which was passive and which was aggressive. Just like going to play group really. You know, you get to colour in with these wonderful coloured pens, you play act arguments. To me I just sit there and think you know, what a waste of time, basically. [Child] sits there and giggles because she thinks it's highly amusing.

There seemed to be some failure to consider the impact of certain interventions on members of the family. In the case from which the above extract is taken, a worker posed a question to the mother in a family session which she regarded as making matters worse:

Respondent M: I was there one day and [the worker] said to me 'is there anything that you can tell me that makes you feel as though her behaviour is 'my fault', and I said 'the only thing that I do feel guilty about is when [child] was first born, I didn't have the mother and baby bond with [this child] … as what I had with the other two'. Because I was so ill, because I had to say this with [child] present, she now says to me 'see, I told you you'd f----d my head up'.

Respondent N: Well I don't feel I can say everything I want to say because I would not want to put [young person] down in front of [young person], if you see what I mean. I mean there are things that I think and feel sometimes that I wouldn't want [young person] to know.

When we asked our sample of 30 families what they thought about the service, almost half mentioned that they liked the worker and just over a third said that he or she was 'easy to talk to'. Two couples commented favourably on their worker's availability and four talked about the fact that the worker had been an active advocate on their behalf. Six families referred to the fact they took the children on trips and gave them a break (although this was not universally appreciated). One respondent simply said that the intervention hadn't worked and therefore did not feel in a position to have an opinion. When asked how they felt generally about the service, just over one third (37 per cent) of respondents were generally positive, one fifth generally negative (20 per cent), and 43 per cent said they had mixed feelings.

When asked what they liked least, over half had nothing to say. Seventeen per cent cited the lack of direct work with the young person concerned and others mentioned feeling ignored (1), let down (1), not knowing what was going on in sessions with the young person (1), and the young person being rewarded for bad behaviour. Although only mentioned by one respondent at this juncture, several families commented on the inappropriateness (as they perceived it) of young people being rewarded for their bad behaviour by being taken out or linked in with activities, etc. when they were being asked to manage their children consistently and according to how they behaved.

> [The CFSS worker] is trying to befriend [the young person] before he actually discusses the problems because [he] is convinced there is an underlying problem that hasn't been discovered yet … With his stepdad … I am very annoyed about this and when he came around I told him we were annoyed with the school … So I told [child and family worker] that and I said to him it is not on – they are undermining my authority by doing that kind of thing – and he said I am in total agreement with you – but every time [worker] picks him up and they go to McDonald's, Burger King, Toys R Us – you name it, he's going – so obviously [worker] hasn't taken any notice of what I have said.

One respondent thought the worker was one-sided.

> Families valued being listened to and having the opportunity to talk things through. Where there were problems, it appeared to stem from *a failure to communicate the rationale behind what was proposed, rather than the work itself.*

Who decided to end the sessions?

We were interested to ascertain the 'transparency' of the decision to end the service, and to gather families' views on the appropriateness of the decision. In eight cases the family did not think the service had ended, or were unclear about this although the service *had* ended. Only four families considered case closure (to the child and family support service) to have been a joint decision between the family and the workers. In two cases, the parents decided to end the sessions and on one occasion the young person took the decision. Families thought the child and family support worker had taken the decision in six instances, otherwise they cited the social worker or the project officer (seven and ten per cent respectively).

Only one third of families said they had been consulted about the decision to end the service. A fifth felt consulted to some extent – in that the family had some awareness that the service was ending, but did not feel consulted as such. Answers depended on how parents interpreted the question.

> Yeh ... I think it would've been nice [to be consulted] ... when she'd come to see us on the last time, you know ... to say ... 'cos she said if I needed her again, I've gotta go through all the social services again [post interview].

Five families did not feel they were consulted at all. Almost half of families did not think the decision to end the service was the right one. Six families said their problems still existed and one family said their problems had got worse. This is rather surprising given that the social work literature usually pay a lot of attention to case closure, stressing the importance of giving service users adequate notice, and managing the process well.

Interestingly, given the challenge of engaging young people, three families gave the fact that the young person was unhappy at the decision as the reason why case closure was not appropriate. Ten families said the intervention should have been longer in order to achieve its aims. Four other respondents said they were unhappy about the outcome. Only five families thought it the right decision because the outcome had been achieved. A further three families thought it the right decision because no more progress could be made. One third of families said they would like to continue receiving a service; one third said they would not. Most of the remainder were still in receipt of services from the social services department.

Reasons for case closure in the closed files

Our attempts to find out if goals were achieved by analysing closed cases were inconclusive. This is important information in itself because it highlights again the difficulties of monitoring and evaluating a service when clear goals are not specified. In general, cases were more often closed for reasons other than the achievement of goals identifiable in the file. The focus on 'process goals' may go some way to explaining this, given that these are not directly concerned with changes in the family. This is what we found in relation to the sample of all 72 families interviewed:

- A quarter of the cases closed to the child and family support service remained open to social services.
- Of those cases which were closed, 24 files (19 per cent) contained no indication of reasons for closure in this final episode.
- Only 11 (9 per cent) cases gave as the reason for closure that goals had been achieved.
- Thirty two (25 per cent) stated 'no further action' and in 19 cases (15 per cent) the reason given was that families refused further help.
- A further five cases (four per cent) were closed because the family changed address.
- Other reasons given were: the involvement of other professional (eight cases) and 'changes of circumstances' (16 cases).

What changes occurred?

We reminded our 30 respondents what they had said their problems were at the time of referral and asked them whether or not these had improved. We also asked them to what they attributed any reason for improvement. Table 10.1 summarises the range of problems these families cited. Clearly there are some differences in the kinds of problems highlighted by parents compared with those highlighted by workers. For example, few respondents saw their problems as arising from inadequacies in parenting. However, there was remarkable similarity in the attention drawn to school problems, relationship problems, and behaviour problems (particularly if one includes aggressive behaviour and dangerous behaviour).

These families appear to be broadly similar to the total sample of families except that rather more parents say their children were not accommodated against their wishes. This may mean that this is a 'tougher' group of parents to satisfy, or that their problems may be more severe. Table 10.2 summarises the extent to which families generally said that each of the problems they had cited had improved.

Table 10.1 Range of problems cited by families

Social isolation	1
Physical ill health (adult)	2
Physical ill health (child)	2
Mental ill health (adult)	1
Mental ill health (child)	4
Substance misuse (child)	2
School	32
Minor offences	6
Major offences	1
Relationship problems (adult and child)	15
Relationship problems (siblings)	7
Domestic violence	1
ADHD / Behaviour problems	9
Aggression	12
Self-harm	1
Dangerous behaviour	6
Sexually abusive towards others	1
Identity problems	1
Parenting	2
Neglect	2
Child NOT accommodated against parent's wishes	4
Child accommodated – rehabilitation more difficult	2
Other	3

Table 10.2 Perceived improvements in families' problems

	%
Improved completely	8
Improved somewhat	34
Stayed the same	35
Got worse	23
Total %	100
N (all problems)	116

We next asked families to what they attributed improvement. Their responses are given in Table 10.3.

Table 10.3 Reasons seen as responsible for improvement

Reasons for improvement	%	%
Not applicable - No improvement	58	
Child and family support services	10	25
Educational service	7	16
Health service intervention	2	4
Change in attitude by young person	11	27
Sorted problems ourselves	1	2
Change in circumstances	3	8
Young male has a girlfriend	1	2
Don't know	5	12
Combination of things	2	4
Total %	100	100
N (all problems)	116	
N ('improvement', all problems)		49

The data in Table 10.3 require careful interpretation, and at best this can only be speculative. For those families who reported improvement (the second column) one quarter attributed change to the child and family support service. Three quarters make other attributions, most notably changes in the attitude of the young person concerned. However, change in attitude by young people may well be attributable to the work done by staff, which so many families said they knew little about. Nonetheless, the trend in the data is towards a conservative estimate of the amount of improvement the service managed to achieve in relation to the problems that families brought with them, and of their role in bringing about what improvements occurred.

These data should be read with the following points in mind:

- This is a small sample, representing approximately one eighth of the families who passed through the hands of the child and family support service during the study period. We have no reason to think they are unrepresentative (given the profile of reasons for referral, demographic data and so on) but we do not know for sure. As indicated above, quite a few parents complained that their children were not placed when they wished them to be.

- People's views of improvement do not always map onto the reality. More generally in the client opinion literature, people overestimate change (see Cheetham and others, 1992) though when it comes to seeing and appreciating improvements in children's behaviour the reverse can be true (see Reid, 1978). It may well be that changes occurred, but were not of a magnitude to stamp themselves on the perceptions of these up-against-it parents.

Generally, however, the picture is not as encouraging as one might hope, and certainly not as hopeful as parents wished. The following quotations provide some examples of the kinds of things parents said, beginning with a parent who clearly regarded the child and family support worker as instrumental in a successful outcome:

> Yeh, definitely ... No, I reckons it's [change] due to [the child and family worker] ... because I personally ... I get more help off of [child and family worker] and she's only been involved the last couple of weeks than I 'ave in the three years I've been with [social worker]. [post interview].

> No, to be honest ... no, no ... I think if she's done it, she's done it on her own and through the help of the school ... you know ... 'cos they've been very ... very very good. [post interview].

> [re: change – negative] I don't know ... it's very depressing for me as well, 'cos it's like he's give up on life, he don't wanna try to do anything any more ... [How are you dealing with that?] Well, I'm on ... tablets ... sleeping tablets at the moment, but I don't take the sleeping tablets all the time ... but I'm going to go back to the doctor's, 'cos I said to the child psychologist, 'it's his concentration span ... it's zilch ... no concentration there at all' ... I said ... 'cos I reckon it might be this ADHD. [post interview].

Quite a few families reported that things deteriorated following their contact with the child and family support service. The reasons parents gave for deterioration, when it occurred, suggested that although they regarded the deterioration as sometimes associated with the child's refusal to engage with the service, it was just as often due to extraneous changes or failures in other services.

Outstanding problems reported by families

We asked our sample of 30 families whether or not they had outstanding problems. Most (87 per cent) said they did.

Table 10.4: Reasons to which deterioration was attributed

Reasons for deterioration	%	%
Not applicable - no deterioration	75	
Intervention not successful	1	4
Child did not engage with service	4	14
Lack of educational intervention	3	11
Lack of primary care intervention	2	7
Change in medication	1	4
General deterioration in child's behaviour	6	26
Change in circumstances	2	7
Don't know	6	26
Combination of things		
Total %	100	100
N (all problems)	110	
N ('deterioration', all problems)		27

- Thirteen families cited school as an outstanding area of difficulty.
- Fourteen mentioned relationship problems (seven between parent and child, five between siblings and two between adults).
- Two parents mentioned ongoing behaviour problems and aggression. These are areas where more intensive, relationship-based cognitive behavioural interventions might well reward effort (see Robin and Foster, 1994; Pinkston and Smith, 1997; Weisz, 1997; Chamberlain and Reid, 1998).
- One family was struggling with a child diagnosed with ADHD. Whilst research evidence currently favours pharmacological interventions, there is also scope to help parents with behaviour management techniques and with personal coping strategies (Zwi and Patel, in press).

Other problems are less obviously the concern of the child and family support service, but may well be a reasonable focus of the longer-term involvement of locality field social workers. Such problems include physical and mental ill health (mentioned by six respondents, four times in relation to the parent) and substance abuse by a child. The other outstanding problems noted by parents were the fact that their son had not (1) or had (2) been accommodated. In the last case, the parent thought that this was making rehabilitation more difficult.

Would you recommend this service?

We concluded the interviews with families by asking whether or not they would recommend the service to someone else experiencing similar problems. The service was valued by the majority of service users. Sixty per cent said 'yes'.

Preventing accommodation in public care

Of the 249 children referred to the child and family support service during the study period, social services records indicate that the majority remained with their carers. Of the 43 children (approximately 17 per cent) subsequently placed in out-of-home care, 27 were still in out-of-home care in July 2000. The remainder had spent periods of time out-of-home ranging from a few days (n=4) to several months (range 2 to 11 months).

These data should be treated cautiously. It is not possible to tell from the data when these placements occurred in relation to the timing of the service. As the service is designed to stabilise families and prevent out-of-home placement, then it does seem reasonable to regard these outcomes as 'failures' on this criterion, although sometimes out-of-home placement may be the optimal outcome for children. Almost as significant is the fact that to reach the figures discussed here took many hours of painstaking work and points (yet again) to the need for better data collection within social services departments.

Of the 152 children whose case files we analysed, 38 had been subsequently placed in out-of-home care during the same period. Given the somewhat longer period for placement (these children all had a longer post-service chance of placement) then this would appear to be comparable. It would appear that the reorganisation did not enable an improvement in placement rates, though of course it could be argued that it has not aggravated the situation.

Only 17 per cent of children whose families had received support from the service during the study period were accommodated in public care, with just under two thirds remaining in care at the end of the study period. This is comparable to the 25 per cent of children whose families had received a service in the preceding two years, and whose cases were now 'closed' to them. However, these data are difficult to interpret as evidence of success or failure. This is because we do not know how many of these children would have been accommodated without a service. This is partly because the study had no control group, but also because it was impossible in all but a few cases, to ascertain even the time period between receiving a service and subsequent placement. Therefore, we cannot be certain that the reasons for eventual placement were related to the inability of the service adequately to deal with the problems referred to it, or to other problems. Finally, some family problems mean that out-of-home placement is the best option for some children.

> This study is not able to provide conclusive evidence about whether or not family breakdown was reduced by the child and family support service.

Preventing school exclusions

Preventing school exclusion was a major aim of this two-pronged service. This study was not primarily concerned with the work of the teachers, but we obtained data on the number of children referred during the study period who were excluded, up to and including July 2000 (therefore comparable to the data for out-of-home placements). Twenty children were excluded during this period. In the absence of information about how many children teachers worked with, it is not possible to comment further on this important area of the service's work. For a variety of reasons (to do with the ability of workers accurately to identify families at real risk of out-of-home placement and with methodological challenges in this area) it is difficult to ascertain, but it seems likely that the prevention of school exclusion was operating at a similar level before reorganisation. Of the 152 children whose case files we analysed, a quarter were excluded from school up until the end-point of the study.

Do these outcomes mean the service is ineffective?

One of the main objectives of the service is to prevent out-of-home placement of children but, as we have discussed earlier, this is difficult to demonstrate (see Pecora and others, 1995) and the best efforts to date suggest that even the most intensive services (including studies in North America) fail to realise this particular goal. This does not mean that the child and family support services are not needed. On the contrary, they appear to be the only major source of therapeutic work available to families and are highly valued by families themselves.

In this study area the agency guidelines are that workers are expected to engage in intensive short-term work with families and children. Some families need long-term help and it may not be reasonable to expect the child and family support service to 'turn around' these families in a short time.

Child and family support services do not hold a case management role or have responsibility for addressing the full range of problems that a family is experiencing. In many cases, and particularly where problems are outside their influence, their role may be more about damage limitation in ensuring that children get a 'good enough' parenting experience, in the knowledge that out-of-home placement is a poor option for most children.

Last, but certainly not the least important, is the timing of child and family support intervention. The evidence from this study, and the wider literature, suggests that preventive work of the kind the social services department expects from the child and family support service would be more effectively and cost-effectively provided at an earlier stage in the development of a families' problems (see Macdonald, 2001; and Macdonald and Roberts, 1996). The next chapter examines this evidence.

> The majority of service users value the help that the child and family support staff are able to offer and would recommend the service to others. In many cases, it is the only help they have received after years of struggle. But the child and family support services are constrained in a number of ways that reduce their effectiveness and many families reported outstanding problems after their contact with the service had ended.

11. Too little, too late? The route to child and family support

When we asked child and family support workers whether there was anything that might undermine the success of their work with children and families, over a quarter (38 per cent) replied that lack of inter-agency co-operation would do so, including the inability to secure appropriate services. For the families they work with, this often has a long history and our research confirmed what other studies and inspection reports have also highlighted in other parts of the UK. By the time families are referred to the child and family support services they have already had a long, and mainly unsatisfactory, history of not getting the help that they need when they most need it. It is in this context that we need to consider the effectiveness of the help provided by the child and family support service in this study area.

This chapter focuses on the families' routes to the child and family support service and charts the patterns of contact that families have had with social services and other agencies.

The first part draws mainly on the analysis of the records of all families who had received a service from the child and family support service and whose cases were closed to that service between November 1997 and November 1998.

All the children featuring in these files were experiencing important changes in their lives, particularly changes of address and family composition. The data here shows the extent of these changes.

The latter part of this chapter refers to data gathered with the families through-out the study period and focuses on the history of their contact with social services.

Patterns of contact with social services

At the time the 152 cases were read and analysed, 90 were closed to social services and 58 remained open to social services although closed to the child and family support teams (data were missing for four cases).

In order to identify the pattern of contact with the department and to track the work undertaken we analysed the files in terms of referral episodes. That is to say, we sought to identify how many times the case was opened and closed (a referral episode). This apparently simple aspiration was immensely difficult to realise. Figure 11.1 provides a picture of the numbers of referrals as recorded by the management information system (CRISSP).

As Figure 11.1 illustrates, upwards of 76 per cent of families had a history of three referrals or more. A significant minority of families had had numerous contacts with social services, some stretching over years. Indeed the majority of files we examined comprised several volumes, sometimes numbering twelve. Information about the opening and closing of cases within the files did not match the

Figure 11.1 Referrals recorded by management information (closed cases)

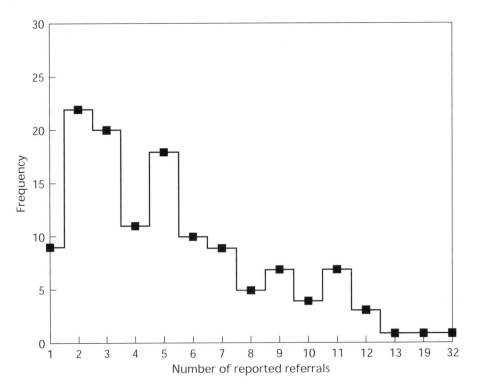

information recorded within the department's management system, and did not always include the information that management required. The episode count used in the following analysis is derived from a judgement based on the content of the file, rather than a reliance on the management information system, unless otherwise stated.

The picture that emerges is as follows:

- half of the cases had one or two episodes
- a quarter had 3 to 5 episodes
- 18 per cent had between 6 and 10
- the remainder had 11 or more.

Of those with more than 11 episodes, one family had 29 identifiable episodes, another 24, one 16, four 13 and one 12.

Although there is no simple relationship between numbers of episodes and length of contact, it is generally the case that the greater the number of episodes, the longer the case was open to social services. Irrespective of time, each episode represents a formal recognition of a need or request for help (or statutory activity) and an opportunity for influence.

Change in children's lives

The children and families had all experienced important changes in their lives during their contact with social services. We look here at three aspects that have implications for the services that might be offered by the CFSS.

Changes of address

The majority of children had had more than one change of address, excluding placements out-of-home. Figure 11.2 indicates the number of moves.

Insofar as changes of address are usually deemed to be serious life events, these children and their families have had a number of upheavals in their fairly short lives. Further, one third of children experienced emergency placements, most three or more (range 1 – 35) and these children all had other placements (i.e. non-emergency and non-respite) as well. All but five of the remaining two-thirds had no placement history.

Figure 11.2 Changes of address excluding placements (closed cases)

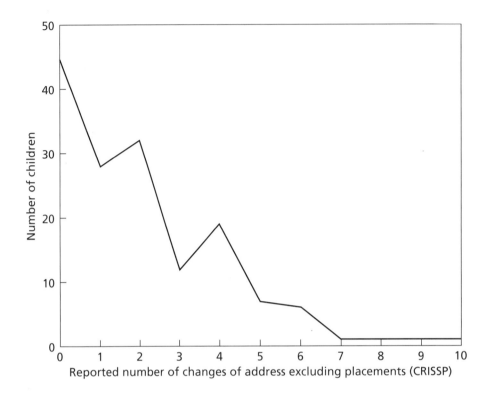

Changes of social worker

According to the information available from the management information system (CRISSP) over half the families had had three or more social workers since their first contact with social services.

Changes in family composition

We tracked changes in family composition across the first 12 referral episodes identifiable in the files. Data regarding changes in family composition are difficult to present. This is partly because of the complexity of the picture, but also because the files do not always provide the information necessary to track changes accurately. That said, there are some clear and important trends regarding the changes that occur in the lives of these children.

- **Step-parents**

  Taking the 'first episode' for all families, 39 per cent of the children referred were from families where there was a step-parent present. Thirty four per cent of children lived in families where there was a stepfather, and four per cent a stepmother (one per cent were living with two step-parents). Forty per cent were from lone-parent families, the majority being single mothers. The remaining children lived with birth mother and father. Throughout most episodes the incidence of step-parents remained between one quarter and one third.

- **Changes in family composition**

  Forty eight per cent of those children with more than one episode have had at least one change of family composition between episodes, and some considerably more. Forty four per cent experienced a change of family composition during an episode. Just over half (52 per cent) of the children in the total sample had had a change either within or between episodes. For those children with more than one episode, this rises to 76 per cent. In the case of 'step-parents' this may underestimate the movement – one should not assume that the step-parents remain the same from one episode to the next.

Implications of all these changes on the work of the CFSS

Such important changes in a young person's life and the lack of continuity that they and their families may have experienced in relation to their contact with locality social workers, further adds to the challenges that child and family support workers face in engaging with them and their parents. The workers often described how difficult this process was, and how it might take many weeks of failed appointments or difficult interviews before they succeeded. It was very easy, and not unusual, for weeks and months to go by with little work being done. This is something which locality social workers and child and family support workers need to address, particularly if the service is to operate at the point at which family breakdown is thought to be imminent. Such turbulence might also indicate the importance of seeking to engage with wider family networks, although this would be a challenging task.

Child and family support workers can do little about changes in social work staff. It might, however, be appropriate to involve locality social work staff more fully in the work undertaken, or at least to liaise with them more closely. When possibilities for joint working with locality colleagues arose, workers spoke positively of these, but such opportunities were rare.

The child and family support workers were acutely aware of the significance of changes in family composition. Reconstituted families present particular challenges to parents and children alike. Complex relationships need to be managed within the new family unit, and between it and families of origin (including grandparents and other kin). Establishing appropriate authority and boundaries is not always straightforward. Much of the success of the new family unit may depend on how previous relationships were ended, how contact is managed, and how children feel about the new adult partner and his or her children. Not handled well, such loss and separation, and the associated conflicts and jealousies that can so easily and understandably arise, can contribute to the development or exacerbation of a range of emotional and behavioural difficulties in children and young people. It can also contribute to heightened levels of verbal aggression and physical violence.

Services designed to prevent out-of-home placement for such children need to be appropriately equipped and resourced to address such problems. Family therapy, relationship counselling and cognitive-behavioural approaches (including family and couples work) are essential components, rather than luxury methods, as they are sometimes deemed to be.

> Many of the families referred to the child and family support service had long-term problems and their lives were characterised by change and a history of contact with social services. This profile suggests a range of service interventions needs to be available to meet the complex needs of these families including, for example, family therapy, relationship counselling and cognitive-behavioural approaches.

We now turn to data from families who were with the child and family support service during the time of our study.

Development of problems over time

For nearly all the families interviewed (88 per cent) there was clear evidence that problems had been developing over a period of time. Early behaviour problems were often noted by parents now trying to handle many of the far more challenging problems that these are frequently associated with, for example, school non-atten-dance, conduct disorders, aggression, delinquency. A mother, whose child has now been diagnosed with ADHD and may have other serious mental health problems, told us:

I struggled on my own for so long without any real help – the number of
times I have had the health visitor up here and I wasn't getting anywhere –
and everyone said you are worrying too much and when he is five and he
goes to school he will be fine – and change – but he didn't – when he is
seven he will calm down – but he didn't – when he goes to junior's he will be
different – but he has just got worse over the years and I could see it coming.

Another parent explained:

I've got onto the school and all I was getting from the school, was go and cry
to your doctor, go and cry to social services and they'll put her into care, but
that wasn't what I wanted. I just wanted someone to sit and listen to how she
was behaving and help me deal with it, because it's not the easiest behaviour,
she does throw things, she's got younger sisters and she beats the living
daylights out of them.

Two of the adolescents, whose families we interviewed, suffered with incontinence
problems, mainly nocturnal enuresis. These problems were long-standing, and have
well-known consequences for children's social development, educational achievement and psychological well-being, yet parents said they had been unable to secure
appropriate help:

Respondent O: She wets the bed. She's 15 years old and she wets the bed.

Respondent P: She's always done that and we never got any help with that.
They always said she'll grow out of it, she'll grow out of it but she never has.

Enuresis was also commented on in the closed files, but was never accompanied
with a plan of how it was going to be tackled, despite the fact that there are readily
available, well-tried and effective interventions.

How did parents feel about this lack of response?

Parents ranged in their responses from being sad to being angry. The following
responses reflect sadly on the fact that the parents felt they needed help but it had
not been forthcoming.

Well prior to [the CFSS worker] getting involved of course, we were
frustrated and very despondent about the fact that we weren't getting
anywhere. We knew there was something wrong with [young person] a long
time ago and it has taken a long time before something happened – and I
find that quite sad really.

> ... in fact one of the [CFSS] social workers has actually got [young person's] file out and read it from front to back – and it is like she said to me he has obviously had a problem since he was very young and all that has been done is he has been pushed under the carpet hoping things would stabilise. And then it just keeps coming up again and again so hopefully they now believe me that something is wrong.

> ... every time they [social workers generally] come in they ask me the same questions all over again ... why doesn't anybody read the notes?

Although some families did not think the CFSS service was the most appropriate service, given their needs, these parents valued this support after so many years without any:

> I asked for help years ago and you sometimes wonder about these profes- sionals and they have got their degrees and yet they can't pick up – I have wondered why service, why this service wasn't offered to us years ago really. Maybe they thought [young person] would grow out of it or I was overreact- ing – I knew I wasn't.

> ... we are learning to deal with him when he is bad and that is where we need the help – we contacted the health visitor, we read books, people with children with similar problems – so we didn't sit back and think – one day he will get better – you will wake up and think everything will be OK.

They also valued the advocacy role that child and family support workers so often took on their behalf, stating that the child and family support staff had managed to open doors that had hitherto remained firmly closed to them.

Previous contact with other agencies

We asked families to tell us what problems they had had in the past, where they had gone for help, and with what outcomes. Just over half of families cited one problem that they had sought help for, with the remainder citing two or more (see Figure 11.3). Most families (80 per cent) said their problems had begun 12 months or earlier (range 1 to 156 months). Many reported repeatedly asking for help from agencies, including social services, which they did not receive, or received but regarded the response as inadequate. Sixty seven per cent reported asking for help from formal agencies at an early stage of their difficulties.

Figure 11.3 Number of problems reported by families

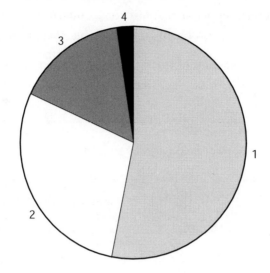

Thirty four families reported two or more problems (13 reported three problems and two reported four problems) which they had sought help for in the past. Since all families cited at least one previous problem, we use this to illustrate the agencies most frequently approached for help. These include: social services (90 per cent), education (68 per cent), the police (44 per cent) primary health care (35 per cent) and housing (31 per cent).

The families appear to rely more on formal support than informal support, with only 40 per cent seeking help from the extended family (probably reflecting the limited availability of grandparents) and only seven per cent (six families) saying they had turned to church or community organisations. Given that the interview actively sought information on both informal and formal sources of support, this is unlikely to be an artefact of the data collection process.

Were problems resolved?

Families reported a mixed response from professionals. Whilst approximately half of the respondents said that they had found the response of professionals helpful, only one quarter reported any improvement in their problems as a result of the help they received. Given the high level of children's problems relating to school, it is worrying that almost one quarter of parents said that they had sought help from education, with no success. Between 25 per cent and 42 per cent of respondents overall said that the responses they had received were unhelpful. Depending on the referral episode, between 55 per cent (most recent referral) and 25 per cent (most distal) commented that their problems continued, but they felt supported.

When asked about the outcomes of the help they had been given by social services, a familiar pattern emerged. Table 11.1 summarises the data for three referrals episodes.

Table 11.1 Family evaluations of help given by social services

Outcomes	Unhelpful	Helpful			NA
		Problem improved	Problem continued but respondent feels supported	Generally helpful (no other information)	
	%	%	%	%	
Referral 1	34	16	35	15	0
Referral 2	29	7	6	6	52
Referral 3	9	3	3	0	85

Although some respondents did feel that the services provided had been helpful, most could not say in what way (column headed, 'generally helpful'). Some were able to say that problems had improved, and others that, although their problems remained pretty much the same, they felt more able to cope due to the support they had received ('problem improved' and 'problem continued but respondent feels unsupported' respectively). No-one said that their problems had been resolved, which is why this category does not appear in Table 11.1. Overall, this is not an unreasonable outcome in complex cases, particularly given the limited resources available to the service, but one might hope that some problems could have been resolved. The data also suggest that help may have not only been too little, but also too late.

When asked about the outcomes of the help they had received from agencies 'across the board', few families reported that their problems had been resolved (one per cent), and only about a quarter were said to have improved. This was a consistent pattern irrespective of what help parents had received. Again, most parents said little had changed but they felt better supported and able to cope as a result of help. What families often said was they needed more help or help on a longer-term basis. Only in 40 per cent of cases was help thought to have been offered for long enough. For example, one respondent said:;

> The team manager – [said] you don't need me you are coping really well
> and that is all they have said to me. That I am coping very well and I am
> thinking but I am not.

Lack of response from key agencies

Overall the data confirm a long history of problems that are not being addressed
by social services or other relevant agencies. At referral to the child and family
support service, many families are already in desperate need of help and for
some this is the first time that anybody appears to be responding to them. It is
not surprising then that the child and family support service is regarded favourably by comparison with social services (see Table 11.2) as we discussed earlier
(chapter 6).

Table 11.2 Relative satisfaction with social services, CFSS and other services

	Completely	Substantially	Quite helpful	Unhelpful	N/A
Other services	7	22	24	44	3
Social Services	13	15	20	46	6
CFSS	21	34	16	13	16

Two thirds of families said they would have welcomed an earlier referral and nearly
half (42 per cent) said that help or support of this kind had previously been
refused by social services.

That said, at the time of interview, only 45 per cent were confident that CFSS was
the right place for them to get help, and 12 per cent were confident that it was not.
Most of the latter were families needing help from mental health services. Forty per
cent of families thought they needed additional services, mainly from the emotional
and behavioural disorder (EBD) team (3 per cent), educational welfare (7 per
cent), and child psychiatry (11 per cent). A few mentioned additional tuition (6
per cent), play schemes and teenage programmes (6 per cent). Eleven families said
they would like access to accommodation for their children and a further 17 per
cent said they would like respite care. Finally, a few families said they would like
social work help (8 per cent) and better liaison with the school (13 per cent).

The need for better and earlier intervention

These data throw some light on three issues that relate to the continuing debate about the need for earlier intervention in child and family support. These are:

■ **Early intervention is likely to be more effective**

Outcome research suggests that for a range of problems early intervention is more likely to be effective than help offered when problems are established and long-term. This is certainly the case in relation to the kinds of problems that social services deal with in their work with children and families. Child behaviour problems are more easy to tackle when children are young than when they are older and susceptible to other sources of influence – such as peer groups – and perhaps involved in antisocial or delinquent behaviour (Macdonald and Roberts, 1996). It is easier to intervene effectively with parents when abuse and neglect are in their early stages than to deal with it once it has occurred (Macdonald, 2001).

■ **Can short-term services address long-term problems?**

If families referred to child and family support services have long-standing and complex problems then it may well be unreasonable to expect them to be able to turn these around in the context of a short-term, non-intensive intervention which is generally restricted to areas of influence within the family itself. A more long-term, multi-faceted approach might have better outcomes.

■ **Do some families respond better than others and why?**

It may be that child and family support services do better with some families than others, and we thought that an examination of the histories of families who had received the service in the course of one year would throw some light onto this. For reasons that are documented in Appendix 3, we are unable to offer extensive or conclusive evidence on this but it is clearly a question that warrants further investigation. This said, there were some examples of problems that could have been solved earlier that were not, for example, nocturnal bed-wetting, child behaviour problems.

The child and family support service was dealing with problems whose origins often went back years rather than months, with missed opportunities for more effective attempts at influence or remedy. This suggests that child and family support services would be more effectively provided as a secondary prevention service rather than a purely tertiary prevention service.

12. Support and professional development

Throughout this report we have highlighted support and professional development issues. Here we focus on two important areas: the need for maintaining an up-to-date knowledge-base and the implications of our findings for support and training.

Keeping up-to-date with research

We asked practitioners what journals they had access to and read regularly, how long they spent reading per week, and which journals they would like to have access to. The majority of staff read *Community Care,* a weekly social care magazine with a wide distribution, but generally 'light' on research content. Six members of staff read the *Journal of Family Therapy,* reflecting a particular area of interest relevant to the work of the service, and an area of practice that some had pursued at post-qualifying level. Beyond this, few key journals in the area of child and family social work were cited as read by respondents, and even fewer were identified as journals that staff would like to have access to (see Table 12.1).

This picture becomes more worrying when one considers how much time most staff said they spent reading journals or other professional literature (see Table 12.2).

Although nine staff reported reading for two hours or more, most read for less than 1.5 hours per week and four never read. On the one hand, this is better than the overall picture provided by a survey of social workers across the whole of the South West region (see Sheldon and Chilvers, 2000) but, given the challenging nature of the work undertaken by the child and family support service, this use of an important source of routine updating and ideas could be improved.

In discussion, the teachers said they felt that the focus on journals was partly responsible for this picture which did not do justice to their reading in terms of keeping abreast of developments in legislation and policy, and the role they played

Table 12.1 Journals read and journals wanted

| | All staff N=23 | |
	Read	Want
British Journal of Psychotherapy	1	
Groupwork	1	
Journal of Family Therapy	6	
Context	2	1
Community Care	16	0
Young Minds	2	0
Professional Social Work	1	0
Research Matters	2	1
Times Higher Educational Supplement	1	0
Child Abuse Review	1	0
Other	5	0

Table 12.2 Hours spent per week reading journals and other professional literature

Hours	0	0.5	1	1.5	2	3	4
N=	4	4	7	2	3	4	2

in helping others to do the same. This is a reasonable point, and social work staff are also involved in this kind of updating. However, we invited staff to say what other sources of information they used, and few made use of this opportunity. Also, journals are an important source of information and there are numerous initiatives aimed at ensuring staff have improved access to them such as the National Institute of Social Work (NISW) library initiatives, the work of the Centre for Evidence-Based Social Services, and Research In Practice (see also Appendix 5).

This picture of the reading undertaken by social workers (and in this case, of some teachers) is not unusual. The reasons are well-known: pressures of work, lack of resources and organisational support.

A number of developments in social work should go some way to improving this situation. The introduction of a three year honours degree in social work as the entry requirement for social work should gradually see an improvement in the overall intellectual ability of staff. Previously considered élitist, this move represents an acknowledgement of the complexity of much of social work, and should help to develop a workforce with a greater appreciation of research and its relevance to practice. This is also evident in the development of the Post-Qualifying Award in Child Care and the requirements it makes of students studying for it. The establishment of the General Social Care Council, and the pressure for social workers to engage in 'continuing professional development', will also help to reinforce the notion that it is important to keep abreast of research and developments in skill if one is to remain 'safe' to practice. This will mean that agencies will need to think strategically about the support they make available to staff to assist them in keeping abreast of the literature, and for encouraging staff to develop their skills and knowledge in areas that the evidence suggest would provide a return of benefit to service users for such investment.

This highlights what may increasingly be a contentious issue. Although the mindset and habits associated with keeping abreast of developments in the field is an essential attribute for evidence-based practice, it will not be sufficient. A critical approach to the quality and relevance of what is being studied is essential, and may pose some difficult challenges to workers whose preferred methods of working appear to lack evidence of effectiveness, and where other, less preferred, methods, show up rather well.

The need for readily accessibly, up-to-date, high quality summaries of research findings will be an increasingly important tool in facilitating an evidence-based approach to practice (see Macdonald, 2001).

> Staff need the time and incentives to keep abreast of relevant literature, particularly outcome research and research which enhances our understanding of the nature and development of core problems. This may require a change in the working culture of child and family support services so that reading and thinking are recognised as essential to professional development.

Support and training

In-service training was mainly practitioner-led in this study, rather than influenced by a strategic or evidence-based view of what skills were required to address the range of problems presented by the service. Several workers mentioned paying their own way, at considerable expense, for courses that were not offered in-house and saw the need to do this as evidence of a lack of investment in staff development by the department.

Some respondents said that the same round of training opportunities came up on a cyclical basis, and that most were not sufficiently targeted at the rather specialist needs of child and family support staff, although this had been promised some twelve months earlier. Others commented on the departmental expectation that sending one or two people on a course would enable them to 'train up' their colleagues – in the view of most respondents, a patently unrealistic and inappropriate idea:

> A couple of us have done some two day courses on brief therapy and the department's view on this is that [we] have learned enough to train the whole for the child and family support service. ... [but] the ones of us that have done it, don't feel confident enough that we've done enough or practised enough...really we're looking for training.

Problems highlighted in this study suggest that qualifying staff are not being adequately trained at present. Teaching the core skills of assessment, monitoring and evaluation would appear to be 'bread and butter' requirements of courses designed to produce qualified social workers. These courses must, in our view, take responsibility for these deficits in knowledge and skill, which are most certainly not confined to this service (see Macdonald, 2001). The introduction of the honours degree in social work, as well as the development of post-qualifying courses and continuing professional development will, one hopes, assist in this. This will only happen, however, if the curricula address these issues thoroughly and robustly.

Based on our findings, child and family support staff need support and training to enhance key areas of practice:

- Assessment
- Goal setting
- Choosing appropriate interventions based on what is required, rather than on what is available
- Articulating the reasons for their choices in clear explicit language, both verbally and in writing
- Monitoring and evaluation.

This study suggests that managers and practitioners need to consider a systematic strategy for continuing professional development to ensure that services as a whole are evidence-based and that individual practitioners have the skills they need to implement appropriate interventions.

13. Conclusions

This study provides insight into the working practices of one child and family support service in the UK. Practitioners shared their thoughts about what they sought to do in working with children, young people and their families, and how they were hoping to achieve their goals. Parents and children talked about how they experienced the service, and how they perceived its aims and objectives, and how it stood in relation to other services, notably field social work. We have much to learn from all groups who contributed. We can learn from points of agreement – for instance, about the need for easier access to such help, and for longer-term assistance in some cases. We can also learn when differences emerge – such as whether interventions should focus on the child or on the family, and the need for workers to explain the reasons for their decisions. The study highlights areas of strength and weakness, and there are lessons here that would help to improve the service's effectiveness.

As we indicated earlier in this report, all the evidence from research suggests that the prevention of out-of-home placement is difficult to demonstrate and the best efforts to date suggest that even the most intensive services fail to realise this particular goal (Littell and Schuerman, 1995). It would be very tempting for cash-strapped managers to read our findings and use some of the more unpromising outcome results to make child and family support services an easy target for saving money. They would be ill advised to do so. The child and family support service appears to be the only major source of therapeutic work available to families and most value it immensely. It is also possible that, in the absence of this service, more children would be placed in out-of-home care with concomitant fiscal and emotional price tags. This study, lacking as it does a control group, cannot say how many children otherwise have been placed in this authority during this time period. More importantly, perhaps, is the lesson from other studies, that family support has a wider remit than simply preventing out-of-home care. It is about improving the quality of life for children, young people and their families. It is about helping families to solve difficult problems, and to cope with difficult times. There is evidence in this study, as with others, that families value this increasingly rare opportunity for skilled help. Although this study cannot provide unambiguous evidence of the effectiveness of the service in these areas, it would be cavalier to ignore the messages that families gave about what they needed and what they valued.

The clear message from our study is that managers and practitioners need to address some of the structural problems that stand in the way of delivering a responsible and accountable service. Child and family support workers cannot make up for the contextual difficulties that surround them, however skilled they may be in their individual practice. Improvements in the way that child and family support is delivered on the ground would then have more chance of success.

The context of the work

The broader effectiveness literature testifies to the difficulty of effecting changes in long-established and complex problems (Macdonald, 2001; Macdonald and Roberts, 1996). Families need help at a time when support might stand an optimal chance of making a difference. If preventive services are to succeed, they must be offered earlier. Further, they must sometimes be available in a more intensive form and for longer periods than is presently the case with much social work help. Precisely the same applies to services aimed at halting spiralling problems in schools.

In other words, local authorities must find a way to provide *timely* help to families, *before* problems become so entrenched that there is little anyone can do. Children should simply not be at the point of exclusion before they are referred to such a service. Providing timely help requires a collaborative approach with education and health, and may well entail rethinking current boundaries, or responsibility and locations of workers (see Bagley and Pritchard, 1998). This local authority has gone some way down this road already in its collaboration with the education department.

It is frankly unreasonable to expect a service with a limited brief (that does not hold a case management role, or have responsibility for addressing the range of problems that a family is experiencing) to turn around problems that have taken years to gestate and develop, particularly in a relatively short period of time. Families themselves were often very vocal with regard to what they saw as the limited and short-term nature of what was an otherwise valued service. There is no reason to think that the findings from this study would not generalise to other areas.

A local authority seeking to improve the effectiveness of its child and family support service should first consider ways of enabling earlier intervention before problems have 'snow-balled' and become more difficult to resolve. In this context *'earlier intervention'* is not synonymous with 'early interventions'. Early intervention programmes, such as SureStart, are designed to maximise a range of developmental outcomes for infants, and to support families with young children in a range of ways. They are preventive programmes which, it is hoped, will impact positively on children and families generally, and in particular, on families from disadvantaged neighbourhoods. If successful, these programmes will undoubtedly reduce the numbers of families who find themselves with long-standing, unresolved problems, and who come to the attention of social services. However, there will be families who fall through the SureStart net, whose problems develop notwithstanding SureStart, or who encounter difficulties after the age range with which SureStart is concerned. Early intervention is about responding promptly to the development of problems, rather than waiting for them to develop to a threshold criterion of severity before families become eligible for services. This applies to health and education, as well as to social services.

The content of the work

There has been relatively little attention given to *what* help is offered to families. This study, along with a number of previous studies, highlights the fact that families have relatively little grasp of what it is that child and family support workers are trying to achieve, or how they are trying to achieve it. There was evidence that such clarity of goal specification and rationale for a programme of work was lacking. Although some staff performed extremely well, this was not commonplace. Not only was it apparently lacking in the working agreements and closing summaries, but staff did not articulate it when asked about what they were hoping to achieve and how.

If social services are to deliver on such policy initiatives as *Quality Protects* (Department of Health, 1998) then social workers will need to become much more skilled at setting clear objectives and specifying outcome indicators that lend themselves to rigorous and transparent monitoring and evaluation. In the absence of such clarity and transparency, it is difficult to ensure high quality decision-making on behalf of children, or to guarantee the best outcomes that we can deliver given our resources. The appropriateness of objectives will, in turn, depend on the availability of high quality assessments. Since this study was conducted, the Department of Health has introduced a new assessment framework, together with schedules for completion, to ensure that this important area of work receives the attention it deserves (Department of Health, 2000). It would be naïve, however, to imagine that the provision of a framework will, in and of itself, result in high quality assessments, however well constructed the framework is. This is because frameworks are only *aides-mémoire*, or organising principles, and tools are only useful when used knowledgeably and purposefully. Neither can ensure that questions will be asked because the practitioner knows why they are important (or not asked because they are irrelevant) or that he or she will know how to interpret the information they collect.

Quality assessments, clear goal setting, and carefully chosen interventions are the hallmarks of an evidence-based approach. The study indicated that there was scope within the agency for developing a more judicious approach to decisions about how to tackle particular problems. This relates not only to individual practitioners, but also to teams and departmental policy:

> Evidence-based practice denotes an approach to decision-making which is purposeful, transparent and accountable, based on a consideration of current best evidence about the effects of particular interventions on the welfare of individuals, groups and communities. (Macdonald, 2000:123)

As this definition suggests, evidence-based work is not simply about *acting* on the evidence. It is about *considering* it in the context of other concerns including, for example, the professional's expertise, knowledge and experience. But it does highlight the need to *know* what interventions are most likely to be effective, with *which* people, facing *which* problems, in *which* circumstances. The organisation of services provided by the child and family support service in this study area generally favoured a counselling approach. For example, workers met with parents and/or children on a weekly of fortnightly basis, to discuss problems and look for solutions. This approach is clearly important, and families valued the opportunities it provided to be listened to, and to explore their problems with workers who were non-judgemental. Our challenge is whether this is a *sufficient* response for many of the problems they were seeking to address. Evidence from families themselves, and from the wider literature, suggest it is not.

Our findings indicate that a wider repertoire of interventions could be made available to families which are designed to match more closely the problems that families and young people are facing, and that might be more effective in resolving their difficulties. This needs to be addressed at a strategic level, as well as on the ground. In this study, for example, child and family support workers were not briefed to engage in long-term support but were expected to effect change in the context of time-limited, short-term session work. Even though this could be extended, the frequency and content of sessions was unlikely to be effective in dealing with the problems some families were dealing with.

The challenges ahead

Enabling practitioners to develop a more judicious approach to decision-making is a challenging task. It begins with qualifying training, where students need to learn the skills of critically appraising the research literature, and making informed decisions. Even with these skills, it is very hard for individual practitioners to keep abreast of an ever-expanding and complex literature. We also need reliable ways of rigorously synthesising research evidence and making it available to practitioners in easily accessible forms. The Joseph Rowntree Foundation has pioneered this approach within social care in the UK, but their experience, like that of the Department of Health, is that even this is unlikely to be sufficient. It requires a shift in organisational culture too, and the development of infrastructures that enable policy and practice in agencies to be responsive to evidence. It will mean not only finding ways of supporting staff in disseminating appropriate material, but doing so in a way that makes it likely to find its way into practice. This entails a number of challenges for organisations. First, it means being prepared to reconsider ways of working. Moving towards early intervention was one example. Enabling staff to work in more concentrated ways is another. Secondly, it means investing in continuing professional development. Knowing 'what works' is of little use if you do not have the relevant knowledge base or skills to implement it.

One of the most encouraging findings of this study was the openness and enthusiasm of the child and family support staff. Here was a group of people highly committed to their work, wanting to help the families referred to them, and doing the best they felt able to do within the constraints placed upon them. Their willingness to have their practice scrutinised was informed by a desire to improve their practice. This is fertile ground for developing an effective child and family support service, and in our experience, this is not uncommon within the profession.

This report is being compiled in a climate of optimism concerning the possibility that the aspirations of staff might be realised. The degree in social work, to be introduced in 2003 and 2004, marks an appreciation, for the first time, of the complexity of much of social work, and the need to have intellectually able people who are competent to practice. The three year degree will make it easier to realise this. The newly established General Social Care Council will register qualified social workers, and other social care staff, and set the conditions for continued registration. This has placed continuing professional development firmly on the agenda, and the responsibility of employers has been reinforced within this. Emphasis is now being placed on social services departments as learning organisations, and these expectations extend to other employers in the social care field. The Training Organisation for the Personal Social Services (TOPSS) has a brief to develop a strategic approach to workforce planning and training. The Social Care Institute for Excellence will promote evidence-based approaches within social work and social care. Finally, there are other developments designed to support policy makers, managers, practitioners and service users in developing an evidence-based approach to practice (see Appendix 5). Together, these developments represent our best chance to date of improving the quality and effectiveness of services to vulnerable people. The study amply demonstrates that the will to provide an effective service is there amongst managers and practitioners. Testimony from the families shows that the need is there. As part of the ambitious, but essential, programme of developing evidence-based policies and practices in social care, we hope that the development of these support structures will help realise grass-roots ambitions for an effective child and family support service.

Appendix 1. Further details about data collection and some of the problems encountered

Data collection

In order to meet the aims of the study, information was collected from five sources. These are described below.

- A content analysis of the records of 152 families who had received help from the child and family support service and whose cases were closed between November 1997 and November 1998 (in relation to that service). These families represented 75% of all those whose cases were closed to the service during that period. The records we examined comprised the entire record of contact between a family and the social services department in relation to children of that family, i.e. excluding records pertaining to parents who themselves had been the subject of social services intervention in childhood. As well as mapping the history of contacts with social services, this part of the study was designed to answer two questions:

  1. Is it possible to identify factors which distinguish families for whom child and family support services fail to prevent placement from those they 'succeed' with, either with regard to the nature and longevity of their problems, or in the services they receive?
  2. Is there evidence of 'missed' opportunities for help that was not provided at the time and that effectiveness research suggests would have been more likely to have succeeded and 'diverted' the family from longer-term difficulties?

  The files were effectively 'interviewed' using a detailed schedule designed to collect and organise information relevant to these questions.

- A pre-test post-test evaluation of the child and family support services. Two sets of data contributed towards this.

- **Interviews with social workers.** We collected information from social workers working within all 249 service users referred to the child and family support service between March and December 1999. Sometimes the referral resulted in a decision that the family was not eligible for service, in which case we asked workers to complete a 'No further action' questionnaire. Information from these sources was collected with regard to 216 of these 249 families. Workers were asked about the appropriateness of the referral, their under-standing of the problems, how they were planning to approach the case, what their aims were and how they were intending to achieve them, how optimistic they were, what factors they thought might undermine the work and whether or not the family needed services which they could not provide, and why. We did not interview teachers involved in particular cases, but talked with social workers and families about their involvement when this was appropriate.
- **Interviews with service users.** We wrote to all families inviting them to partici-pate in an interview. Seventy two families agreed to be interviewed, and 30 of these were interviewed both shortly after the referral to the family centre and following the completion of services. Difficulties with this area of the study are discussed below.

- Background interviews with all family centre staff, to elicit general information which we thought might influence service delivery and shed light on the find-ings, e.g. training and experience of staff, levels of support, preferred ways of working and available skills.
- An analysis of the working agreements, reviews and closing summaries of those cases referred to the service, including those where we had not been able to interview the family.
- An analysis of data available from the management information system to iden-tify what had subsequently happened to children in relation to placements or exclusion from school, whether or not cases remained opened to social services or were closed, whether or not the child's name was placed on or removed from the Child Protection Register.

Engaging families

Responses from families was very poor throughout the study, but exceptionally so in the early months. Eventually we decided to offer a choice of gift vouchers (value £10) to families per interview, and this undoubtedly improved our response rate, but too late in the project to secure a large sample of pre- and post-test interviews. It also meant that some of the 'first interviews' were conducted with families who had already received a number of contacts with the service. Given the scope of the interview this was not thought to be too worrisome, so they were included in the pre-post sample.

Technically it would have been possible to have a pre-post test sample of 39 of the 72 families available for interview. However, due to a number of problems, we succeeded in interviewing only 30 families near the point of service entry and again at termination of service. Some of these problems were due to the difficulties we had in contacting families, and realising an interview. However, this was also due to the fact that in a number of cases it was some time (i) before a meeting was set up between the CFSS and a family, (ii) between that meeting and the first session, and (iii) because in many cases the workers did not pass the project 'pack' to families. Reasons for the late delivery of the 'pack' ranged from simple 'forgetfulness':

> I have had a few recently, I haven't managed to get off the ground very quickly because a social worker's been on holiday or something. Then I finally get to do this home visit, to meet these people properly, having only met one person, forget the pack don't I, you know? And this week I'm actu-ally seeing them for a session on Thursday and I am meeting somebody again for the first time tomorrow so I've put two packs in my diary in the hope that you know somewhere along the line I, 'cos it's like just another thing to remember.

to a reluctance to do so, lest it fracture what was perceived as a delicate worker–client relationship, or increase pressure on an already 'up-against-it' family:

> I think if we've starting work with a family that, that maybe for whatever, you know from wherever, sort of like they are not very keen to work but they have said that they will and you know things are maybe a little bit difficult it just feels like another piece of bureaucracy.

These problems were exacerbated by the fact that families often did not return slips and/or were difficult to arrange to interview. This was a problem encountered by the research team which mirrors a problem experienced by workers themselves. Staff emphasised that very often it takes immense persistence to engage families, to establish trust and rapport, as well as there being very practical challenges like securing attendance at appointments, persuading and helping families to keep to plans. This may go some way to explaining workers' reluctance at times to 'add' to the apparent demands placed on families.

Appendix 2. Further details about the families who were interviewed

Data were gathered from interviews with the 72 families referred to the service during the study period. Of these 72 families, 30 were interviewed at two points in time: shortly after referral and then after the case was closed to the child and family support service.

Timing of the interviews

We interviewed families after they had seen the worker on a couple of occasions. This was intended to leave sufficient time for workers to secure a clear and detailed picture of a family's problems, to have determined the aims of the work and how they hoped to achieve them, and also how optimistic they were about a successful outcome. The period was generally between two and eight weeks, but in a number of cases it was considerably longer because of the delays in clients receiving information about the project. Respondents could not always recall how many sessions they had had, or over what period of time. We in fact interviewed seven families where the service had been terminated. Of these, one family had refused the service offered; two had not 'engaged' with the workers; three families decided the service was no longer needed (either because a more appropriate service had been made available or the problem had been resolved) and one family refused a service. For this reason, the numbers of respondents for whom we have certain pieces of information varies somewhat.

The children and their families

Of the families interviewed in the study, the majority of children were male (72%) and aged 13 to 15, somewhat higher than the service as a whole. Their ages ranged from 6 to 17 years. The majority of children were white. Nine children lived with both birth parents. Thirty six lived with either their mother (33) or their father (3)

and 12 lived in reconstituted families. The remaining six lived with grandparents
(1), other relatives (4), or a stepmother (1). Thirty five per cent of the children
were the oldest in their families, another 30 per cent being the second eldest. Of
the 63 children who had siblings only 44 per cent shared the same parents.
Although relatively few children were living with both parents, 35 per cent were in
touch with birth fathers living outside the family (41 per cent were not), 5 per cent
were in contact with mothers living outside the household (8 per cent were not),
and 17 per cent were in touch with step-parents (12 per cent were not).

Mothers and fathers were predominantly in their 30s (ranges 26 to 52 and 30 to 59
respectively). They were mostly white English (57). Four mothers were African
Caribbean, one mixed parentage and one Scottish. This was broadly representative
of the local population, where 9 per cent of the population are from minority
ethnic groups. We sought to make comparisons with the referrals to social services
overall, but this was not possible due to the fact that such data were not available.

Almost half the mothers had left school at age 16 or earlier with no formal qualifications. A further 30 per cent had some qualifications at CSE level. Only one
mother had A-levels and one had attended adult education. Sixty per cent of
mothers were unemployed. Of these, ten were caring for dependants and eight
were disabled. Of the 21 fathers for whom we have information, the majority had
no formal qualifications, but most were employed.

The number of fathers for whom particular kinds of information is available varies.
This occurred for a number of reasons. Some mothers did not have information
relating to absent fathers, and a number of mothers were reluctant to discuss absent
fathers on account of relationship problems between them. We asked families about
significant others who were not living in the household, not least of all because a
number of workers had indicated that the complexities of working with reconstituted families was a major challenge. A few families mentioned ex-partners as
significant extra-family contacts, but generally fewer than expected. It is possible
that this reflects the high number of families who identified previous domestic
violence and/or relationship problems between parents living apart as problems.
Maternal grandparents were important sources of support to many families (30 per
cent cited maternal grandfathers and almost 40 per cent cited maternal grandparents), but few families reported contact with paternal grandparents.

Forty-four families lived in local authority housing and a further seven lived in other
kinds of rented accommodation. Only 12 families were owner-occupiers. Twenty two
per cent of families (16) had only been in contact with social services for six months
or less, but the remainder had been known for longer periods.

Management information indicated that:

- all but six of the children whose families we interviewed had been referred on more than one occasion, with most having three or more referrals;
- child protection investigations had been instigated in respect of approximately one fifth with most having just one investigation (range 1 to 4); and
- 17 children had been the subject of a child protection case conference, 10 of them on more than three occasions (range 3 to 19).

CRISSP does not differentiate between new case conferences or review case conferences, but judging from the fact that in 11 of these cases there is only one recorded child protection investigation, then the majority are probably reviews. The names of eight children were currently on the child protection register, and a further six had been registered in the past. Those children registered were registered at the time of referral to social services, three for physical abuse, one for emotional abuse and four for a combination of the two. Judging from the fact that of the 168 working agreements that we analysed, nine children were stated as registered, it is possible that this is an underestimate, or minimally that there is some inconsistency between data on CRISSP and data in the files (compare analysis of closed cases). Eighteen children had been placed in out-of-home care, half of them on more than one occasion.

At the time of interview, nine children were looked after. Six of the children who were accommodated were with foster carers and three were in residential care. These last three had been placed since referral.

Appendix 3. The limitations of data from the closed files

Relying on data from files is inherently problematic. Leaving aside problems of the often chaotic organisation and illegibility of material recorded in social services files (well documented in public inquiries) it is not easy to determine whether something has not been done, or whether there is simply no record of its having been done. For this reason, amongst others, we do not presume to present our data as a secure judgement on social work practice in relation to these 152 families. It is the most accurate picture that can be pieced together from the files and the file is the *only* record available of what was done or not done, with or to whom, within what timescale and with what outcome. Improving the quality of data placed on files is an important task.

Limitations of the data about service provision

We had hoped that our research design would give us a more complete picture of service provision, especially through our analysis of the closed files. Unfortunately we were limited by the quality of data on the files. With regard to service provision we hoped to do the following:

- to document the profile of service responses to the range of problems dealt with by the teams;
- to explore the extent to which services were offered at an *optimum* time, such as whether or not families received help at an early enough point in the development of their problems to maximise the chances of success and to prevent deterioration;
- where research evidence is available regarding 'what works', to explore the appropriateness of services offered to families.

In order to do this we developed a very elaborate schedule which took some considerable time to complete and code. Sadly, it proved to be largely a waste of time. Although it was possible to identify 'concrete services' such as play groups or referrals to other agencies, it was generally not possible to find, in the files, any record of work undertaken specifically by social workers (or indeed other professionals) to address the problems that families were presenting. Family work was sometimes mentioned, and counselling (in the sense of 'talking through') was implicit in much of the recording. However, family therapy, relationships counselling, behaviour therapy, anger management, child management and so on were rarely, if ever, mentioned, and only occasionally discernible within the record.

Appendix 4. Evaluating the quality of assessments

	Assessment						
34	Was an assessment undertaken?	Yes		No		Doesn't say	
35	If Yes, by whom?	SW		CFSS		Doesn't say	
36	Is there a written assessment on the file?	Yes		No		Doesn't say	
37	Was it a 'comprehensive assessment'?	Yes		No		Doesn't say	
38	Where was it undertaken?	Home		FC		Other: state	
39	How many weeks/sessions did it take?						
40	Does it contain a social history?	Yes		No		Doesn't say	
41	Does it provide an account of the development of the family's problems?	Yes		No		Doesn't say	
42	Is a theoretical perspective evident?	Yes		No		Doesn't say	
43	If there is, please identify:						
44	Is reference made to research on causes of problems?	Yes		No		Doesn't say	
45	Is there a clear problem formulation?	Yes		No		Doesn't say	
46	Is there a clear plan for assistance?	Yes		No		Doesn't say	
47	Does it address the problems identified?	Yes		No		Somewhat	
48	Is reference made to effectiveness research?	Yes		No		Doesn't say	
49	Are reasons given for proposed plan?	Yes		No		Doesn't say	
50	Are alternatives considered?	Yes		No		Doesn't say	
51	Estimated degree of 'logical fit'						
	Completely		Substantially		Somewhat		Not at all	
52	Was the rationale for the plan explained to parents?	Yes		No		N/A	
53	Was the rationale for the plan explained to children(?)	Yes		No		N/A	

Appendix 5. Resources for evidence-based knowledge: useful websites

Campbell Collaboration (http://campbell.gse.upenn.edu/)

Cochrane Collaboration (http://hiru.mcmaster.ca/cochrane/)

Economic and Science Research Council (http://www.evidencenetwork.org/newsletter.asp)

Joseph Rowntree Foundation (http://www.jrf.org.uk)

References

Bagley, C and Pritchard, C (1998) 'The reduction of problem behaviours and school exclusion in at-risk youth: an experimental study of school social work with cost-benefit analyses', *Child and Family Social Work*, 3, 4, 219–26

Bandura, A (1977) *Social Learning Theory.* Englewood Cliffs, NY: Prentice Hall

Biehal, N, Clayden, J and Byford, S (2000) *Home or Away? Supporting young people and families.* Joseph Rowntree Foundation/National Children's Bureau

Bridge Child Care Development Service (1995) *Paul: Death through Neglect.* Islington Area Child Protection Committee

Chamberlain, P and Reid, J B (1998) 'Comparison of two community alternatives to incarceration for chronic juvenile offenders', *Journal of Consulting and Clinical Psychology,* 66, 4, 624–33

Cheetham, J, Fuller, R, McIvor, G and Petch, A (1992) *Evaluating Social Work Effectiveness.* Open University Press

Davies, C, Morgan, J, Packman, J, Smith, G and Smith, J (1994) *A wider strategy for research and development relating to personal social services.* HMSO

Davies, M (2001) *The Blackwell Companion to Social Work.* Blackwell Publishers

Department of Health (1988) *Protecting Children: A Guide for Social Workers Undertaking a Comprehensive Assessment.* HMSO

Department of Health (1994) *Children Act Report 1993.* HMSO

Department of Health (1998) *Quality Protects: Framework for Action.* Department of Health

Department of Health, Department of Education and Employment (2000) *Framework for the Assessment of Children in Need and their Families.* The Stationery Office

Feldman, L (1991a) 'Evaluating the impact of intensive family preservation services in New Jersey' *in* Wells, K and Biegal, D E (1991) *Family preservation services: Research and Evaluation.* Newbury Park, CA: Sage

Feldman, L (1991b) *Preserving families: Evaluation resources for practitioners and policymakers.* Newbury Park, CA: Sage

Fischer, J (1973) 'Is casework effective?: A review', *Social Work*, 18, 5–20

Fraser, M W, Pecora, P J and Haapala, D A (1991) *Families in Crisis: The Impact of intensive Family Preservation Services.* New York: Aldine de Gruyter

Gibbons, J with Thorpe, S and Wilkinson, P (1990) *Family Support and Prevention: Studies in Local Areas.* National Institute for Social Work

Hess, P M, Folaron, G and Jefferson, A B (1992) 'Effectiveness of family reunification services: an innovative evaluative model', *Social Work,* 37, 4, 304–11

Kazdin, A E 'Conduct disorder across the life-span' *in* Luthar, S S, Burack, J A, Cicchetti, D and Weisz, J R *eds* (1997) *Developmental Psychopathology: Perspectives on Adjustment, Risk and Disorder.* New York: Cambridge University Press

Kazdin, A E, Siegel, T and Bass, D (1992) 'Cognitive problem solving skills training and parent management training in the treatment of antisocial behavior in children' *Journal of Consulting and Clinical Psychology,* 60, 733–747

Littell, J H and Schuerman, J (1995) *A synthesis of research on family preservation and family reunification programs.* Office of Assistant Secretary for planning and evaluation (DHHS)

Macdonald, G M (1990) 'Allocating blame in social work', *British Journal of Social Work,* 20, 525–46

Macdonald, G M (1998) 'Promoting evidence-based practice in child protection', *Clinical Child Psychology and Psychiatry,* 1, 71–85

Macdonald, G M 'Evidence based practice' *in* Davies, M *ed.* (2000) *The Blackwell Encyclopaedia of Social Work,* Blackwell

Macdonald, G M (2001) *Effective interventions in child abuse and neglect: an evidence-based approach to planning and evaluating interventions.* John Wiley

Macdonald, G M and Roberts, H (1996) *What Works in the Early Years?* Barnardo's

Macdonald, G M and Sheldon, B (1992) 'Contemporary studies of the effectiveness of social work', *British Journal of Social Work,* 22, 615–43

Macdonald, G M and Williamson, E (2001, in preparation) *A systematic review of the effectiveness of family preservation services.*

Marsh, P and Triseliotis, J (1996) *Ready to Practise? Social Workers and Probation Officers: Their Training and Their First Year of Work.* Avebury

NHS Centre for Reviews and Dissemination (2000) *Evidence from systematic reviews of research relevant to implementing the 'wider public health' agenda.* Prepared by: Contributors to the

Cochrane Collaboration and the Campbell Collaboration and the NHS Centre for Reviews and Dissemination, with support from the NHS R&D Programme. August

Parton, N ed. (1997) *Child Protection and Family Support: Tensions, contradictions and possibilities.* Routledge

Pecora, P J, Fraser, M W and Haapala, D A 'Client outcomes and issues for program design' *in* Wells, K and Biegal, D E (1991) *Family preservation services: Research and Evaluation.* Newbury Park, CA: Sage

Pecora, P J, Fraser, M W and Haapala, D A (1992) 'Intensive home-based family preservation services: an update from the FIT project', *Child Welfare*, 71, 2, 177–96

Pecora, P J, Fraser, M W, Nelson, K E, McCroskey, J and Meezan, W (1995) *Evaluating Family-Based Services.* New York: Aldine de Gruyter

Pinkston, E M and Smith, M D 'Contributions of parent training to child welfare: early history and current thoughts' *in* Lutzker, J R ed. (1997) *Handbook of Child Abuse Research and Treatment.* New York: Plenum Press

Rachman, S J and Wilson, G T (1980) *The Effects of Psychological Therapy.* 2nd edn. Pergamon Press

Rees, S and Wallace, A (1982) *Verdicts on Social Work.* Arnold

Reid, J B (1978) *A Social Interactional Approach to Family Interactions. Volume 2: Observation in Home Settings.* Eugene, Oregon: Castalia Publishing

Reid, J B ed. (1979) *A Social Learning Approach to Family Intervention: Volume 2: Observation in Home Settings.* Eugene, Oregan: Castalia Publishing

Reid, W (1994) 'The Empirical Practice Movement', *Social Services Review,* June, 165–84

Reid, W and Hanrahan, P 'The effectiveness of social work: recent evidence' *in* Goldberg, E M and Connelly, N eds (1981) *The Effectiveness of Social Care for the Elderly.* Heinemann

Robin, A L and Foster, S L (1994) *Negotiating parent–adolescent conflict: a behavioural family systems approach.* New York: Bruner Mazel

Rose, W (1994) 'An overview of the development of services – the relationship between protection and family support and the intentions of the Children Act 1989'. *Department of Health Paper for the Sieff Conference,* 5 September, Cumberland Lodge

Rutter, M, Giller, H and Hagell, A (1998) *Antisocial Behaviour by Young People.* Cambridge University Press

Rzepnicki, T L, Schuerman, J R and Johnson, P R 'Facing uncertainty: reuniting high-risk families' *in* Berrick, J D, Barth, R and Gilbert, N eds (1997) *Child Welfare Research Review: Volume II.* New York: Columbia University Press

Sanders, R, Colton, M and Roberts, S (1999) 'Child abuse fatalities and cases of extreme concern: lessons from reviews', *Child Abuse and Neglect,* 23, 3, 257–68

Schuerman, J R, Rzepnicki, T L and Littell, J H (1994) *Putting families first: An experiment in family preservation: Modern applications of social work*. New York: Aldine de Gruyter

Schwartz, I M, AuClaire, P and Harris, L J 'Family preservation services as an alternative to the out-of-home placement of adolescents: the Hennepin County experience' *in* Wells, K and Biegal, D E (1991) *Family preservation services: Research and Evaluation.* Newbury Park, CA: Sage

Sheldon, B (1978) 'Theory and practice in social work: a re-examination of a tenuous relationship', *British Journal of Social Work,* 8, 1, 1–18

Sheldon, B and Chilvers, R (2000) *Evidence-Based Social Care: A study of prospects and problems.* Russell Sage Publishers

Smith, A F M (1996) 'Mad cows and ecstasy: chance and choice in an evidence-based society', *Journal of the Royal Statistical Society,* 159, 3, 367–83

Social Services Inspectorate (1986) *Inspection of the supervision of social workers in the assessment and monitoring of cases of child abuse.* Department of Health

Social Services Inspectorate (1994) *Evaluating child protection services: Findings and issues – inspections of six local authority child protection services 1993: Overview Report.* SSI

The Children Act 1989. HMSO

Truax, C and Carkhuff, R (1967) *Towards Effective Counselling and Psychotherapy,* Chicago: Aldine

Weisz, J R 'Effects of interventions for child and adolescent psychological dysfunction: relevance of context, developmental factors, and individual differences' *in* Luthar, S S, Burack, J A, Cicchetti, D and Weisz, J R eds (1997) *Developmental Psychopathology: Perspectives on Adjustment, Risk and Disorder.* New York: Cambridge University Press

Wells, K and Biegal, D E (1991) *Family preservation services: Research and Evaluation.* Newbury Park, CA: Sage

Wierson, M and Forehand, R (1994) 'Introduction to Special Section: The role of longitudinal data with child psychopathology and treatment: preliminary comments and issues', *Journal of Consulting and Clinical Psychology,* 62, 5, 883–6

Zwi, M and Patel, S (2001*) Parent-training interventions in Attention-Deficit/Hyperactivity Disorder.* The Cochrane Library, Issue 2, Oxford: Update SoftwareMacdonald, G M (1998)

Index